Magic Internet Money

A BOOK ABOUT BITCOIN

Jesse Berger

ISBN (Paperback): 978-1-7771284-0-1
ISBN (e-Book): 978-1-7771284-1-8
ISBN (Audio): 978-1-7771284-2-5

Edited by: Catherine Leek of Green Onion Publishing
Interior Design and Layout by: Kim Monteforte of Kim Monteforte Graphic
    Design Services
Cover Design and Illustrations by: Daphne Mariano

This book is dedicated
to my role models:

Mom – for your courage,
your wisdom, and for always
looking on the bright side.

Dad – for your poise, your
resolve, and for teaching me to
play both sides of the ball.

CONTENTS

WHAT IS MONEY?

"Fix the money and you fix the world."

MARTY BENT, *TALES FROM THE CRYPT* PODCAST

Money is always and everywhere a social phenomenon in the sense that any change to its value or usefulness affects our behavior, because it constitutes half of every transaction that perpetuates society. Given this, why do we seldom question the merits of our current monetary system? Why do we allow it to function without justification or consequence?

Perhaps our attention is so squarely focused on quantity – on having enough money – that we regard its qualitative properties as a foregone conclusion. In overlooking it as an instrument that works best when finely tuned, we chase it like a fish does bait, unaware of the fact that our meal comes with strings attached. This blind spot is the greatest obstacle preventing us from seeing how modern money is negatively affecting our wealth and well-being.

Today, money is controlled by masters who, obscured behind a veil of prestige, pull its strings like a puppeteer, leading us astray like the pied piper. Operating under the guise of promoting prosperity, they deceive us into discounting their dismal track record, which perpetuates economic inequality by continuously diluting the value of our money, affecting how we use our time and efforts.

Enter Bitcoin. It was purpose-built to restore the uplifting capacity of money and challenge the proficiency of the legacy monetary system. It incentivizes collaboration by acting as an impartial and mutually beneficial medium that, if increasingly chosen as the preferred basis for commerce, has the potential to generate remarkably positive economic and social changes.

To understand how, *Magic Internet Money* explores a variety of related subjects, describing them in broad strokes. It assesses what money is, how it works, why it is useful, and why it has value. It examines how money could best function for the benefit of everyone – equally and for all time – and why Bitcoin is best suited for this purpose.

One of the special facets of Bitcoin is that it has no throne. No king or queen can assert their dominion, no CEO can determine its agenda, and no government can legislate its activities. With no central authority, the responsibility to manage, promote, and protect its livelihood resides with its users, each of whom understands and values Bitcoin on their own terms. As a community, they openly share knowledge and ideas about Bitcoin, some of which will be echoed in the pages ahead.

If after reading this book you find yourself curious to learn more, I have included a list of resources at the end. There, you will also find a list of key terms that you can reference should you require clarification on any of their meanings, but you do not need to understand them before starting.

Personally, I first heard about Bitcoin in 2011 while working in the investment industry. I watched from the sidelines as its price soared from under $1 to $30, leading me to believe that I missed the boat. Only in 2017 did I finally try using it for the first time, and that proved to be a necessary step in deepening my appreciation for it. If I could share any advice regarding Bitcoin, it would be that it is never too late to begin experimenting.

Professionally, I studied economics and philosophy prior to starting out as a retail banker and investment adviser. During that time, as I grew my knowledge of the financial sector, I made a few trips to the *World Series of Poker*, which helped me better understand how to put risk and reward into perspective, and to be accountable for my choices. I then went on to earn my MBA, where I led the winning team of *The Economist*'s global investment case competition, defeating over 25 schools from around the world. Afterwards, I worked as a finance and market research consultant, before becoming a certified blockchain professional and venturing out on my own into the wonderful world of Bitcoin.

Born and raised in Toronto, Canada, I was first alerted to the faults in our current monetary system and misconceptions in popular economic theory in the aftermath of the Global Financial Crisis, right as my career was beginning. It prompted me to contemplate the question "what is money?" After 13 years, what follows is my attempt to provide an answer. I hope you find it agreeable.

Jesse Berger

CHAPTER 1

NARRATIVE

1.1   ONCE UPON A TIME

"Storytelling reveals meaning without committing the error of defining it."

HANNAH ARENDT, POLITICAL
THEORIST & PHILOSOPHER

What is it about a great narrative that can be so memorable? So meaningful? So enduring?

It's a community of narrators reciting a story time and time again, asserting the same virtues and wisdom, using different voices and emphases. Readers and storytellers recall conflicts faced by protagonists and invoke connections to their own situations. The more persuasive the story, the deeper the personal bond it forms with its audience.

With the passage of time, the reverence of its status can be cemented through the reiteration of defining characteristics that are timeless. In this way, a compelling and consistent narrative can become legend.

To tell of Bitcoin is to tell of just such a legendary tale, defined by a single, constant characteristic – stoicism.

Bitcoin, as a peer-to-peer electronic monetary system, epitomizes stoicism by exhibiting the absolute and unyielding ability to continuously perform exactly the task for which it was designed, no matter the circumstances. This perpetual determination is the beating heart of Bitcoin's potent narrative.

1.2 FROM SEED TO SAPLING

"A well-thought-out story doesn't need to resemble real life. Life itself tries with all its might to resemble a well-crafted story."
ISAAC BABEL, AUTHOR, JOURNALIST & PLAYWRIGHT

The story begins with a carefully considered idea – an experiment – to test a new operating framework for a computer network that could become universally recognized as honest and useful money. This concept had long been incubated by "cypherpunks," an online advocacy group for privacy-enhancing technologies, but Bitcoin was the first to give it life.

When Bitcoin emerged, it did so on the Internet, everywhere and all at once, with no strings attached. Due to its inventive use of cryptography, software, and engineering, the network has now been running for over 11 years with virtually zero downtime. As the monetary phenomenon at the center of its own economy, it is being nurtured by a growing and enthusiastic community.

Like everything else in the world, Bitcoin faces hardships. Whether technological, social, or economic in nature, the resolutions to these hardships are part of its continuous evolution, and act as data points in its ongoing evaluation.

From bleeding edge technology developments to profound social corollaries to sensational price swings, its results to date are encouraging. Considered as a single system, Bitcoin's functionality, community, and economics integrate seamlessly. As a new form of money, it produces a powerful allure that continuously inspires the evolution of its utility and value.

1.3 DOWN THE RABBIT HOLE

"I'll tell you a secret. Old storytellers never die. They disappear into their own story."

VERA NAZARIAN, FANTASY & SCIENCE FICTION AUTHOR

For all intents and purposes, Bitcoin is a highly dependable global public good. It is an accessible and interconnected communications network, which anyone can use to transfer, validate, and protect proprietary data.

Support for the network has always been rooted in the fundamental interests of its users. In this sense, it's like a passion project, a labor of love. Since Bitcoin never received any funding or special privileges, it is constantly proving its worth in order to earn its keep.

Having originally produced a monetary revolution, Bitcoin is also at the forefront of change in many other domains. Like a lighthouse on a foggy night, the closer you get to it, the more its surroundings are revealed. From this clarity, interest in its abilities tends to grow, leading to the experimentation and evaluation of its applications. In this sense, Bitcoin can be explored like a choose-your-own-adventure novel, and the best way to understand it is to keep choosing a new path to follow.

Those attempting to learn about Bitcoin often compare the experience to tumbling down the rabbit hole as in *Alice in Wonderland*. It's like stumbling around in a parallel universe. You cannot make sense of it all at once, and the only way to grasp it is to go through it.

CHAPTER 2
ORIGINS

2.1 IMMACULATE INCEPTION: SATOSHI'S VISION

"They manifested, like a flame. They weren't really from anywhere. The conditions were right and they came into being ... I found them in here. Like flowers in a wasteland. Profoundly wise. Unimaginably naïve. They were spectacular."

EDWARD KITSIS & ADAM HOROWITZ, *TRON: LEGACY*

On October 31, 2008, Satoshi Nakamoto published the Bitcoin white paper,[1] a manifesto for monetary independence. The nine-page paper unveiled the technical details and rationale for a robust new system that envisioned using digital signatures to authorize the transfer of scarce electronic coins. The transactions and whereabouts of every fraction of every coin would be documented on a public ledger that would be freely available for download and inspection.

The name Satoshi Nakamoto is a pseudonym. Satoshi's true identity is unknown, and that anonymity has forever shrouded Bitcoin in mystery. This background lends a cosmic quality to Bitcoin, since it arrived quite unexpectedly, like a meteor from cyberspace – its true point of origin unknown. Crashing into the World Wide Web, it created a crater in our perception of money, with the force of its impact distributing its remnants across the Internet to be discovered like a natural resource.

The consequences of its arrival are striking. It directly confronts long-held monetary dogma, and the transparency of its network means that its activities can be observed, measured, and analyzed, allowing anyone to contemplate the disruptive nature of Satoshi's vision.

2.2 GENESIS: A NEW HOPE

"Behind this mask there is more than just flesh. Beneath this mask there is an idea … and ideas are bulletproof."

ALAN MOORE, *V FOR VENDETTA*

Satoshi first ran the Bitcoin software on January 3, 2009, when the network was launched in the public domain. This initial instance of Bitcoin is known as the "Genesis block."

Within the Genesis block, Satoshi embedded the following message: *"The Times* 03/Jan/2009 Chancellor on brink of second bailout for banks."

Here, Satoshi commemorated the network's launch by highlighting a timely concern about the moral hazards inherent in our global monetary and banking systems, which were, and still are, on the brink of fallibility. This message is relevant to Bitcoin because it was specifically developed as a systematic upgrade – to be a principled monetary alternative for the 21st century and beyond.

In late 2010, almost 2 years after its launch, Satoshi stopped communicating publicly about Bitcoin in chat forums, and also stopped contributing to ongoing software development. Without further input from its sole creator, Bitcoin would have to find its own way in its pursuit of monetary relevance.

In the post-Satoshi era, Bitcoin has continued to be relentlessly productive. With each passing day, it infringes further into the territory of the legacy monetary system, inspiring the study of uncommon knowledge about money, and fanning the flames of its public discourse.

▲ Cover of *The Times*, January 3, 2009.

▼ Raw hexadecimal output of the Genesis Block.

```
00000000  01 00 00 00 00 00 00 00  00 00 00 00 00 00 00 00   ................
00000010  00 00 00 00 00 00 00 00  00 00 00 00 00 00 00 00   ................
00000020  00 00 00 00 3B A3 ED FD  7A 7B 12 B2 7A C7 2C 3E   ....;£íýz{.²zÇ,>
00000030  67 76 8F 61 7F C8 1B C3  88 8A 51 32 3A 9F B8 AA   gv.a.È.Ã^ŠQ2:Ÿ,ª
00000040  4B 1E 5E 4A 29 AB 5F 49  FF FF 00 1D 1D AC 2B 7C   K.^J)«_Iÿÿ...¬+|
00000050  01 01 00 00 00 01 00 00  00 00 00 00 00 00 00 00   ................
00000060  00 00 00 00 00 00 00 00  00 00 00 00 00 00 00 00   ................
00000070  00 00 00 00 00 00 FF FF  FF FF 4D 04 FF FF 00 1D   ......ÿÿÿÿM.ÿÿ..
00000080  01 04 45 54 68 65 20 54  69 6D 65 73 20 30 33 2F   ..EThe Times 03/
00000090  4A 61 6E 2F 32 30 30 39  20 43 68 61 6E 63 65 6C   Jan/2009 Chancel
000000A0  6C 6F 72 20 6F 6E 20 62  72 69 6E 6B 20 6F 66 20   lor on brink of
000000B0  73 65 63 6F 6E 64 20 62  61 69 6C 6F 75 74 20 66   second bailout f
000000C0  6F 72 20 62 61 6E 6B 73  FF FF FF FF 01 00 F2 05   or banksÿÿÿÿ..ò.
000000D0  2A 01 00 00 00 43 41 04  67 8A FD B0 FE 55 48 27   *....CA.gŠý°þUH'
000000E0  19 67 F1 A6 71 30 B7 10  5C D6 A8 28 E0 39 09 A6   .gñ¦q0·.\Ö¨(à9.¦
000000F0  79 62 E0 EA 1F 61 DE B6  49 F6 BC 3F 4C EF 38 C4   ybàê.aÞ¶Iö¼?Lï8Ä
00000100  F3 55 04 E5 1E C1 12 DE  5C 38 4D F7 BA 0B 8D 57   óU.å.Á.Þ\8M÷º..W
00000110  8A 4C 70 2B 6B F1 1D 5F  AC 00 00 00 00            ŠLp+kñ._¬....
```

12

2.3 OPEN SOURCE: THE INTERNET STRIKES BACK

"We see Bitcoin as potentially the greatest social network of all."

TYLER WINKLEVOSS, VENTURE CAPITALIST

Bitcoin would not be possible without the Internet. It lets computers communicate freely with each other by using standardized data transmission formats and processes, known as "protocols."

If the Internet is the protocol for the free exchange of information, then Bitcoin could be thought of as the protocol for the free exchange of value.

Bitcoin's software is open source, meaning that anyone can download, use, inspect, modify, and enhance it. Developers can propose and review code for new features, or build applications and businesses to enhance user experience and boost network adoption.

Protocols act as common bonds between computers running the software, connecting them to form a "network." The Bitcoin network's activity, openly visible to all, attracts participants to coalesce around it, becoming a "community."

Recognizing that Bitcoin is simply an agreeable basis for interaction is key to understanding why it continues to thrive. The software is willingly shared by many people, using many devices, in many regions around the world. This makes it extremely difficult to stop because it is simultaneously stored and operated everywhere, and because its global community has incentive to keep it running.

2.4 Consensus: The Return of Integrity

"Bitcoin is a game where everyone watches everyone else to make sure nobody cheats."

Jameson Lopp, CTO of Casa

To maintain the trustworthiness of the network's incentive mechanism, and to mitigate counterfeiting or hacking, Bitcoin insists on its own brand of collaboration, which is commonly known as "consensus." Bitcoin's consensus mechanism solves a computing problem known as the Byzantine Generals Problem, which stems from a lack of trust.

In short, the problem states: multiple parties must agree on a single strategy in order to avoid failure, but the communication channels needed for coordination are susceptible to corruption. How do the parties reliably synchronize their efforts?

Bitcoin forges consensus through "proof-of-work", which is a technique in cryptography that makes valid transactions costly to create and difficult to falsify, yet easy to verify. Like a mathematical equation, it takes effort to decipher without knowing the solution, but once given, the whole formula can be easily understood. For the Byzantine Generals Problem, this means that all parties can reliably coordinate their efforts with one another because authentic communications can be positively validated, with any corrupt messages easily detected and omitted. This breakthrough led *The Economist* magazine to dub Bitcoin's consensus solution as "the trust machine."[2]

Thinking in terms of game theory, consensus renders cheating an ineffective strategy because it ensures that adversaries can only benefit if they abide by the rules. In this way, the integrity of Bitcoin is elevated to practically guarantee honor, even among thieves.

2.5 E-MONEY: FULLY CHARGED

"As a rule, there is nothing that offends us more than a new kind of money."

ROBERT LYND, *THE PLEASURES OF IGNORANCE*

Money is an instrument. It is the embodiment of value that takes the form of an agreeable medium in order to quantify the productive use of time, skill, and energy. Almost anything can be money, but not everything should be. In a perfect world, the correlation between the value of our productivity and money would be evident and commensurate.

This idealistic notion led 19th century luminaries, like inventor Thomas Edison, futurist Buckminister Fuller, and industrialist Henry Ford, to endorse the idea of money created from energy. They believed energy – the driving force of all life – to be a suitable basis for money because it is objectively measurable, widely producible, and inherently valuable. However, due to the constraints of efficiently sending and storing energy, this idea was never realized.

A century later, cypherpunks, like David Chaum, Adam Back, Wei-Dei, and Nick Szabo, launched their own digital currencies, trying to solve lofty monetary issues relating to privacy and trust using cryptography and computer networks. Though their experiments did not succeed in their own rights, they laid the foundation for a successor.

Bitcoin is considered a remarkable achievement because it is the realization of many classic and modern ideals for money. By converting chaotic energy into an orderly monetary system, it accurately compensates costly effort with value, and through proof-of-work, it methodically documents irrefutable evidence of its own authenticity. In this sense, Bitcoin is like catching lightning in a bottle, since it forges and secures trustworthy money from energy.

2.6 Fixed Supply: The Promised Land

"The nature of Bitcoin is such that once version 0.1 was released, the core design was set in stone for the rest of its lifetime."

Satoshi Nakamoto, Creator of Bitcoin

The Bitcoin network does not actually consume energy itself, but computer processing power, which is fueled by energy. This consumption process is known as "mining," and it performs two very valuable tasks. First, mining enables Bitcoin's native monetary units, called "bitcoins," to be found and spent, and second, it provides security to the network.

By way of computational effort, miners compete to settle the next block. Each block is like a page of transactions in a ledger, and the Bitcoin protocol ensures that one miner wins a block approximately every 10 minutes. The winning block is then broadcast to the network so it can be verified by participating computers known as "nodes," which bond it to all previous blocks, creating a sequenced digital chain – the complete ledger of all transactions.

Winning miners are rewarded with new coins called "block rewards," as well as that block's transaction fees. Solidly etched into its code, block rewards are issued on a predetermined schedule, decreasing by half every 4 years until Bitcoin reaches its fixed supply limit of 21 million coins, which is expected to occur near the year 2140.

The asymmetry of mining – high effort for inputs and effortless verification of outputs – deters cheating since false blocks result in nothing but wasted resources for dishonest miners. This creates a virtuous circle whereby miners must compete on a level playing field to earn rewards, and the act of competing secures evidence of rewards' scarce existence. In this way, mining enforces the foundational promise made by Bitcoin – to only ever issue 21 million coins – a strict limit that very credibly differentiates it from any other known money.

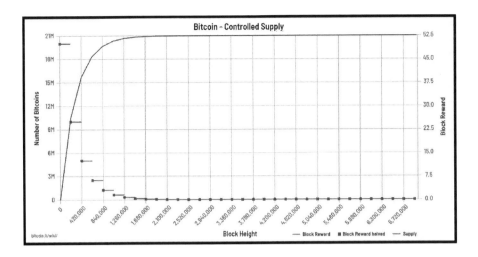

Bitcoin's Supply Issuance Schedule: Bitcoins are issued at a decelerating rate. The higher the block height (the number of blocks between any given block and the Genesis block), the lower the rate of issuance. Bitcoin entered the 4th epoch of block rewards (6.25 bitcoins per block) in May 2020 when it reached the 630,000-block mark, and it will enter the next epoch at block 840,000, which is expected to be mined in the year 2024.

Source: https://en.bitcoin.it/wiki/Controlled_supply

2.7 In Memoriam: The Shrine of Satoshi

"I volunteer! I volunteer as tribute!"

Suzanne Collins, *The Hunger Games*

All bitcoins can be divided into fractions as small as one hundred millionth of a coin, or 0.00000001. This smallest unit of account is known as a "sat," in honor of Satoshi. As of May 2020, over 18.3 million of the 21 million bitcoins have been mined, meaning that 87% of all coins are currently in circulation today.

In August 2018, Bitcoin trading and research firm BitMEX estimated that Satoshi mined roughly 600,000 to 700,000 bitcoins, or approximately 2.85% to 3.33% of the total supply.[3] Although all wallet balances are visible on the network's public ledger, this figure can only be estimated because wallets are pseudonymous. No names are associated with wallets by design, because identity is not a prerequisite of participation. Regardless of the owner's true identity, those holdings have remained untouched to this day. At this point it's more likely than not that they will never be spent.

Over time, those coins have become a testament to Satoshi's humility and restraint. Had they been spent, Satoshi could have been accused of being greedy, using a privileged first-mover advantage for personal gain. Instead, by effectively sacrificing those coins, they have endowed Bitcoin with a halo effect, which conceptually hovers over the network, positively influencing perception of its integrity. As long as those coins remain untouched, they will stand as a timeless monument to the ethos of Bitcoin, conferring an aura of altruism, and adding verifiable legitimacy to its compelling claim as principled and incorruptible money.

CHAPTER 3
MONEY

3.1 THE ROOT OF ALL GOOD

"So you think that money is the root of all evil ... Have you ever asked what is the root of money?"

AYN RAND, *ATLAS SHRUGGED*

Money is a means to an end – to facilitate the efficient allocation of resources in society. It was first invented to allow barter economies to grow beyond their natural limits by acting as a liquid, precise, and valuable medium for commerce. Fundamentally sound money allows for fair and fluid trading by accurately measuring prices, creating conditions for productivity to improve, and generating economic growth, like a rising tide lifting all boats. If defective, however, money can have the opposite effect, confusing trade markets by distorting the pricing mechanism, causing valuable resources to be misallocated, thereby weakening an economy's efficacy.

Some economists with a preference for free-market ideology, most notably those from the Austrian school of thought,[4] have long questioned the ability of the legacy monetary system to beneficially allocate resources and stimulate growth. Although it has served for many decades, entrenching itself into the global economy, it shows signs of defect, misuse, and fragility. Having studied these deficiencies, Satoshi equipped Bitcoin with attributes and abilities intended to overcome the current system's shortcomings, and to compete on a universal level for monetary value and mindshare.

By virtue of its existence, Bitcoin publicly challenges our underlying assumptions about money, as well as the role of the gatekeepers tasked with determining its governance policies. To find out how, it must first be understood what makes for sound money.

3.2 SOUND MONEY REDEFINED

"Sound money is the equivalent of scientific integrity: the system must not permit the manipulation of data after the experiment has taken place."

GEORGE GILDER, *THE SCANDAL OF MONEY*

Money can be considered fundamentally sound and ideal for long-term use if it has credibility and integrity. To do this, it must meet six key criteria, which were coined in principle by the Greek philosopher Aristotle over 2,300 years ago.

1. Money should be durable, so it can be stored without deteriorating over time.
2. Money should be portable, so it can be easily transported across space.
3. Money should be divisible, so it can be split into smaller quantities and assembled into larger ones.
4. Money should be scarce, so its supply remains low or, better yet, limited.
5. Money should be fungible, so that authentic units are easily recognizable, interchangeable, and difficult to counterfeit.
6. Money should be costly, so that the means by which it is produced or acquired establishes a basis for value.

With these attributes, money could fulfill its three primary functions.

1. **Medium of exchange**: Agreeable method of payment for the sale, purchase, or trade of goods and services.
2. **Unit of account**: Standardizes the measurement of value in order to accurately determine pricing for commerce.
3. **Store of value:** Has beneficial and desirable qualities that can be reliably preserved over time.

3.3 A Very, Very Brief History of Money

"The promise given was a necessity of the past: the word broken is a necessity of the present."

Niccolo Machiavelli, Renaissance
Diplomat & Philosopher

Money has taken many forms throughout history – from seashells to salt to stones and more. For hundreds of years leading into the 20th century, gold was the standard for global money because, more than anything else, it most closely met the criteria of sound money, and people generally found it agreeable for that purpose. As such, nations held gold in reserve to support the value of their currencies. If they wanted to create more currency, they had to acquire more gold, ensuring that the currency's values were justified because gold vouched for its integrity.

In 1971, with gold-backed US dollars serving as the world's reserve currency, the United States unilaterally severed the convertibility of dollars to gold.[5] From that point onwards, all global currencies started a journey into unchartered territory, unsupported and unrestrained by any credible reserve asset. In effect, the sound characteristics that had been conferred by gold were traded for expediency, giving countries free reign to undermine the integrity, and therefore the value, of their currencies, regardless of the consequences.

Unlike gold, trust in this new system was not agreed upon, earned, or proven – it was appropriated. This is the grand illusion of the modern monetary system. Like waving a magic wand, an executive decree made a trusted golden foundation vanish, and replaced it with the printing presses and paper promises of "fiat" currency.

3.4.1 WHAT THE FIAT! WHO SAID SO?

"The first lesson of economics is scarcity: There is never enough of anything to satisfy all those who want it. The first lesson of politics is to disregard the first lesson of economics."

THOMAS SOWELL, ECONOMIST & SOCIAL THEORIST

A "currency" is a promissory note that is meant to be redeemable for some promised value – for a credible monetary asset. In the past that promise was gold.

A currency can be labelled "fiat" when its promised link to monetary value is broken, or was non-existent in the first place, but its use is still insisted upon by authorities. As it stands today, fiat is the standard for all state currencies.

All major global currencies – dollars, euros, yuan, yen, pounds, francs, etc. – are fiat in nature because they are not redeemable for any monetary asset, they are issued by central authorities, and their use is insisted upon by law. Under the fiat system, the value of a currency is derived, in part, from the relative trustworthiness and stability of the issuing nation, meaning its government's fiscal responsibility and political reputation. Other considerations, such as a currency's supply and demand in trade markets, also factor in.

Without a sound asset against which to pledge its integrity, currency supplies can be increased at will, diluting their value without consent from its citizenry and enabling governments to write checks they cannot honestly cash. In Latin the word "fiat" translates to "let it be done" or "it shall be." In other words, the world uses fiat because "they said so."

3.4.2 WHAT THE FIAT! CIRCULAR LOGIC

"The curious task of economics is to demonstrate to men how little they really know about what they imagine they can design."

FREDERICK A. HAYEK, AUSTRIAN ECONOMIST

A central authority, usually an unelected and opaque entity such as a central bank, is required in the governance of a fiat currency. This governance determines monetary policy, which typically employs two primary tools: 1) supply – the amount of currency deposited into and withdrawn from the monetary system – and 2) interest rates – the cost of borrowing for the banking system.

Fiat monetary policy agendas differ from country to country. Generally speaking, though, they target stable prices and a stable rate of economic growth. While stability may seem like a noble endeavor, it highlights the curious relationship of cause and effect between money and economics.

Like putting the cart before the horse, changes to monetary policies constantly alter the scales that measure value, because policies are variables that affect the quality of money. These changes impact economic activity, which is then used to justify further policy changes. This vicious cycle of policy impacting the economy, which then impacts policy again, is the Achilles' heel of fiat money because it is a system based on improvisation. Like a storm cloud looming ominously over the economic horizon, it generates uncertainty, casting doubt on its long-term outlook.

Over the course of many decades, mainstream economic theory has conditioned us to believe that monetary policy must be flexible in order to accommodate the ebbs and flows of an economy. Furthermore, we are given no choice but to trust that the leaders of our central banks are wholly benevolent and wise in their determination of those policies. This system leaves much to be desired in our pursuit of prosperity since its effects do not clarify, but rather confuse, our ability to clearly perceive value.

3.4.3 WHAT THE FIAT! EMPTY PROMISES

"Debts and lies are generally mixed together."

FRANCOIS RABELAIS, RENAISSANCE
WRITER & PHYSICIAN

The extent of uncertainty and doubt that central bank policies are capable of producing has been on full display since the onset of the Global Financial Crisis.[6] The world has been showered with very low interest rates and inflated currency supplies, enabling enormous debts to be accumulated. This situation has weakened both the soundness of global currencies and broad conviction in future economic prospects.

Without credible assets as restraining factors, fiat currencies have and continue to be created and spent with minimal regard to repercussions. The normalization of increasing currency supplies combined with very low interest obligations has reduced the importance of debt repayment considerations, encouraging widespread lending and speculation. By running up debts without discipline, the world perilously borrows unearned savings from its future. Despite historical precedents suggesting that those bills always come due, these short-sighted policies have become the model upon which the world is increasingly and erroneously dependent for economic expansion.

So, in an economy that is careless in its consideration of future consequences – where currency issuance is inexpensive, rising in spite of its ability to gauge value, and where debts can be incurred without regard to repayment – why should fiat currency be considered valuable? What promise does it hold? Practically and historically speaking, fiat money's fundamental value proposition is suspect, and its promises are seemingly empty.

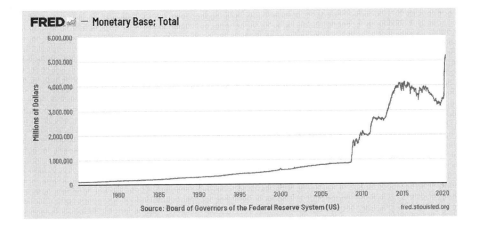

Source: Board of Governors of the Federal Reserve System (US)   fred.stlouisfed.org

US Monetary Policy: As the world reserve currency, the US dollar settles the majority of global trade, and its monetary policies could be considered a proxy for all fiat currencies. Since the Global Financial Crisis, supply has been increasing at an unpredictable rate, and interest rates have been flatlining. As of May 2020, with the US national debt at a staggering $25 trillion (over $75,000 per American), it is worth asking – on what basis is the fiat monetary system credible?

Source: US Federal Reserve

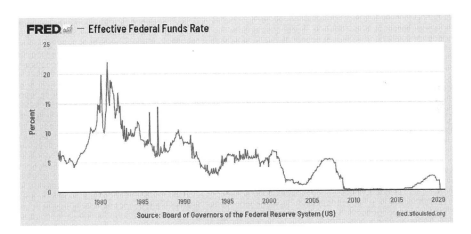

Source: Board of Governors of the Federal Reserve System (US)   fred.stlouisfed.org

3.5 FIAT FUNCTIONALITY

"The root problem with conventional currency is all the trust that's required to make it work. The central bank must be trusted not to debase the currency, but the history of fiat currencies is full of breaches of that trust."

SATOSHI NAKAMOTO, CREATOR OF BITCOIN

Today, fiat functions as money because it satisfies the three primary functions – albeit tenuously.

Medium of exchange: Legal tender laws require that, to varying degrees, fiat be used within a country for commerce. Legally enforcing fiat assures a high degree of acceptability, even if it is somewhat constrained by borders and red tape.

Unit of account: Fiat is moderately useful because it is easily divided, counted, and is commonly accepted, but its unstable and unpredictable monetary policies blunt the precision with which it can accurately measure value over time.

Store of value: With no sound underlying basis, fiat currency has value due to little else besides the general expectation that it should be valuable. This value is at all times presumed and subject to change based on its unknown future policies.

The authorities relied upon to uphold the integrity of fiat currencies and promote economic welfare regularly undermine the confidence markets are asked to place in them. The questionable agendas and outcomes of their policies cast a long shadow of doubt over the fundamental soundness of fiat money. The economic consequences of their actions will be explored further in Chapter 4.

3.6.1 Bitcoin on Point: Think Different

"The waste of plenty is the resource of scarcity."
THOMAS LOVE PEACOCK, ENGLISH NOVELIST

Unlike fiat, Bitcoin is not a promissory note. Bitcoin is its own foundational monetary system.

Unlike fiat, Bitcoin cannot have its supply diluted. Network consensus ensures that its supply issuance is predictable and its limit is fixed.

Unlike fiat, Bitcoin is not restricted by geographical or legal limitations, and it does not insist on its own use. Its use is entirely voluntary.

Unlike fiat, Bitcoin has no central banking or governing authority, and no economic mandate. No agenda is required because its monetary policy was scheduled in advance and revealed to the public the moment it was launched.

Bitcoin's value, a contentious topic at this juncture due to its exuberant volatility, is and always has been open for discovery by the market. It has never been assumed or taken for granted.

Bitcoin could be considered trustworthy because transactions are fully verifiable, and it could be considered stable because the entirety of its supply schedule is known in perpetuity. If, like fiat, Bitcoin were to be valued based on its trustworthiness and stability, then any demand it generates will necessarily have to square off against its fixed supply, which, it should be noted, is mined at an appreciable cost.

3.6.2 BITCOIN ON POINT: MARKET RATE

"The most important single central fact about a free market is that no exchange takes place unless both parties benefit."

MILTON FRIEDMAN, ECONOMIST
& POLITICAL PHILOSOPHER

There are no interest rates to influence the cost of Bitcoin, which is neither free nor fixed. There are land, labor, and capital requirements needed to mine it and maintain the security of the network. Bitcoin miners, though, do not determine these costs for themselves like central banks and governments do with interest rates. Instead, the cost of Bitcoin is determined by a single, variable factor – demand.

How does this work? The computational difficulty of mining, which impacts the amount of energy that must be expended, directly affects costs. This difficulty is programmed to self-adjust every 2 weeks depending on the amount of mining resources joining or leaving the network. When there is more computing power directed towards mining, the difficulty and energy requirements are higher; when there is less power, energy and difficulty requirements are lower.

This means that Bitcoin is harder and expensive to mine when demand is high, but easier and cheaper to mine when demand is low. This mechanism for clearly identifying and adjusting the intersection of demand against its fixed supply results in the timely depiction of its production costs on the open market. In other words, Bitcoin is its own free market for determining its value as money.

3.6.3 BITCOIN ON POINT: IN GOOD TIME

"Patience is a conquering virtue."

GEOFFREY CHAUCER, MEDIEVAL POET & AUTHOR

Unlike fiat, Bitcoin cannot respond to economic turmoil by increasing supply or reducing interest rates. In stoic fashion, it can only adhere to its predetermined issuance schedule, and then simply let the aggregate effort of markets determine its value. The absence of the ability, and therefore the temptation, for any central bank or government to manipulate money protects its credibility. Furthermore, this condition assures that Bitcoin, as a standardized scale for measuring value, is always precise.

Unlike fiat, which mortgages its integrity through reckless policies to satisfy mandates for short-sighted economic objectives, Bitcoin skews behavior in the opposite direction, pushing concern towards the future. Its fixed supply means that once spent, more bitcoins are not easily created or earned. Users must therefore tame any sense of urgency and defer gratitude by saving money, selectively deploying it to maximize their return, which often means prioritizing long-term outcomes. By directly aligning the capacity to spend with the benefits of spending, Bitcoin encourages the productive use of capital while also promoting patience as a virtue.

Some schools of economic thought view Bitcoin's fixed supply as a problem, but there is no law of economics or nature insisting that a money supply must be flexible for an economy to grow, or that money and state are mutually exclusive. In the absence of central administration, market forces would simply compel monetary value to either accrue or diminish against its fixed supply in response to economic developments.

In these formative years of Bitcoin's existence, volatility in its monetary value can and should be expected. However, if its value proposition and status in global markets matures, then over an extended timeline its relative volatility should subside.

3.6.4 BITCOIN ON POINT: THE HARD LINE

"Money is good for nothing unless you know the value of it by experience."

P.T. BARNUM, SHOWMAN & POLITICIAN

The hardness of Bitcoin's fixed supply limit, its predictable issuance schedule, and its free market costs of production are all competitive advantages that it has over fiat money.

When choosing between competing monies, the money with a stronger value proposition tends to disappear from circulation, getting saved because users prefer to spend their weaker money first. This is a monetary principle called "Gresham's law."

The degree to which this principle will hold for Bitcoin depends on public perception. Perception is influenced by our awareness, understanding, and trust in Bitcoin as a sound and viable monetary option. Its ability to acquire and retain this status will depend on it staying true to the hard-coded monetary policies that uphold its credibility.

So, will Bitcoin keep its foundational promise and uphold its stated monetary policies? Its history of consistently adhering to protocols despite having no central authority, strictly observing its fixed issuance schedule, and maintaining a perennially free market for its production costs, all operating virtually without interruption for over a decade, confidently suggests that it will.

3.7 BITCOIN FUNCTIONALITY

"It's not about making money with bitcoin. It's about making bitcoin money."

FERNANDO ULRICH, MONEY, BANKING
& TECHNOLOGY ANALYST

Bitcoin functions as money because it adheres to the three primary functions.

Medium of exchange: Although not commonly used in commerce today, it can be traded on demand, so its design is suitable for this purpose. In the future, greater understanding and trust in its benefits, combined with improved ease of use, will increase the fluidity and likelihood of its acceptance.

Unit of account: Bitcoin is always accurately authenticating each and every fraction of coin, and its supply is strictly limited, making it very useful as a finely tuned and enduring scale for the measurement of value.

Store of value: Bitcoin currently behaves more like a speculative store of value than a lasting one, since its value proposition is not assured in public markets. In time, its sound attributes and unique utility may propel preference for its use, resulting in the maturation and stabilization of its value.

Despite having launched only 11 years ago, there is reason for cautious optimism regarding Bitcoin's prospects for becoming universally recognized as honest and useful money. It faithfully adheres to the characteristics demanded of sound money and, as will be discussed further in the next chapter, it can efficiently allocate resources and curtail waste by promoting shrewd decision-making, acting as an engine for growth.

CHAPTER 4
GROWTH

4.1 THE ROOT OF ALL GROWTH

"The use of a single medium is highly advantageous for the same reasons that a money economy is superior to a barter economy: it makes exchanges possible on an incalculably wider scale."

ALAN GREENSPAN, FORMER US
FEDERAL RESERVE CHAIR

Bitcoin's price has unwittingly become a focal point of its existence. Due to its relative nascence, the breadth of its exchangeability and depth of its liquidity are still experiencing growth spurts, leading to its famous price volatility. This ancillary effect of its real-world utility draws both ire and awe from financial markets, who, like everyone else, simply want to find out how and if Bitcoin can benefit them.

The answer to this question is surprisingly straightforward – Bitcoin can benefit everyone if it becomes widely recognized and used as money. How so? By standardizing a public scoreboard to assess value today and into the future, fundamentally sound money acts as fertile soil in which trade and investment can flourish. This produces positive changes to social and economic behaviors, leading to greater overall prosperity and wealth, in addition to growing its own value.

It should go without saying that money has an enormous impact on our overall well-being, but explaining the rationale can be complicated. This chapter will therefore describe how monetary characteristics affect personal decision-making and, consequently, the way that we grow.

4.2.1 THE VALUE OF PRICE: CAUSE & EFFECT

"What economic calculation requires is a monetary system whose functioning is not sabotaged by government interference."

LUDWIG VON MISES, AUSTRIAN ECONOMIST

If money is a cause, then economy is its effect. Money measures value, resulting in a price to evaluate the costs and benefits of trade, determining if any given exchange is "worth it." When money is the value protocol tying a community into a network, it becomes the basis of an economy.

Pricing is of paramount importance to the economic process. It occurs as the result of agreement between community members, reflecting their unique insights into resource abundance or scarcity, factors of production, and personal preferences. In a sense, prices are like air traffic controllers for an economy, coordinating when and where value is taking off, landing, waiting, or canceled. They convey economic knowledge, which informs decision-making regarding the timing and amount of money to be deployed for any given objective.

When money is agreeably exchanged, it leads to additional productive capacity and the creation of valuable goods or services, otherwise known as "growth." Growth lets us enjoy a higher standard of living, which we could call "prosperity," and to maximize the value of our possessions, which we could call "wealth."

Considering the crucial role that price signals play in directing growth, it stands to reason that the most desirable outcome for money should be the timely and accurate portrayal of prices, because prompt and proper prices lead to more informed agreements – a necessary condition of mutually beneficial outcomes.

4.2.2 THE VALUE OF PRICE: SIGNAL & NOISE

"Let's not repeat what created our troubles. I want real growth, not a series of bubbles. Stop bailing out losers. Let prices work. If we don't try to steer them, they won't go berserk."

JOHN PAPOLA & RUSS ROBERTS, ECONSTORIES.TV

Under the fiat monetary system, the premise of accurate pricing is rejected. Instead, prices are influenced by a central steering committee on an unwinnable quest for stability. While targeting stable prices and stable growth may seem admirable, it is a fool's errand because economies are not static, but dynamic. Whether due to human nature, innovation, or cyclical or natural events, economies are always changing, and these fluctuations result in periods of expansion and contraction, which prices are meant to reflect.

By constantly tinkering with monetary policies, central banks destabilize the scale for gauging prices, confusing our ability to detect authentic value. Unable to be accurately perceived, prices can become delusional, as if the air traffic controllers had their signals crossed. This renders fiat unfit as a unit of account because it leads to misguided investing and wasteful spending, which is the air that fills financial bubbles and causes unnecessary economic turmoil. In essence, the only thing that fiat's forced stability stimulates is a forced illusion.

Bitcoin, meanwhile, accepts value as it comes. Like a fearless honey badger, it does not concern itself with externalities. Its fixed and transparent supply means the settings of its scale are calibrated for pinpoint precision, so it can excel as a measure of value. Whether prices are volatile or stable, it stoically accepts them as they come – reflecting life's changing values and preferences – and dutifully relays the knowledge they signal, making Bitcoin a far superior unit of account.

4.3.1 Time Is Money: Scarcity Abides

"Many people take no care of their money till they come nearly to the end of it, and others do just the same with their time."

Johann Wolfgang von Goethe,
Writer & Statesman

In a very real sense, time is money. Like money, time can be invested to create something of value, and can be traded if the price is right. The inherent scarcity of time in life inspires us to use it efficiently because, if wasted, time cannot be artificially re-created.

Money and time, though, have historically had a tumultuous relationship. Time almost always ravages the value of money primarily because some authority mismanages its supply, devaluing it with reckless abandon. From the debasement of the Roman denarius coins' silver content in the 3rd century to Zimbabwe's peak inflation rate of 79,600,000,000% in the 21st century, the same story recurs in different forms throughout the ages – central authorities fund their exorbitant privilege by producing baseless currency. At first this distorts the price signal mechanism and impedes trade, but as the rate of supply growth increases it eventually destroys its own value and, subsequently, its economy.

Throughout much of history, the value of gold has endured because its supply is not centrally controlled. Its natural scarcity rubs salt in the wounds of fiat currencies past and present, serving as a constant reminder that when it comes to money, there is a correlation between supply scarcity and value longevity. If money and time are to finally find harmony and create lasting economic benefits, money must abide by the principle of scarcity prescribed by time and end artificial supply inflation.[7]

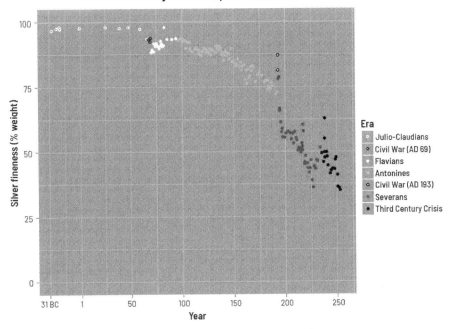

Fineness of early Roman imperial silver coins

Monetary Debasement: History is littered with examples of empires and nations that abused their monetary privileges by artificially increasing supply. Given that all past instances of fiat money end in ruin, it is worth asking – on what basis is our current monetary system built to endure? Why is this time different?

4.3.2 Time Is Money: Use It Wisely

"Nowadays people know the price of everything and the value of nothing."

OSCAR WILDE, POET & PLAYWRIGHT

Today, these lessons go unheeded. As if suffering from a case of mistaken identity, central banks push for stability instead of accuracy, mistaking the prince for the pauper. Moreover, they appear to suffer from amnesia, inflating currency supplies instead of limiting them, dubiously repeating the mistakes of their failed predecessors. Inevitably, these policies affect our time preference, which in economics refers to our behavior relative to the perceived value of money over time.

The longer an inflatable currency is held, the higher the risk that its value will decrease, destroying the impetus to build savings for the future. Instead, it encourages us to deploy currency sooner than later, either by spending it on consumables, or by investing it and taking on unwanted risks. This orientation towards instant gratification, known as "high time preference," often leads to impulsive and ill-advised behavior and, as a result, wasted resources. In a word, it creates inefficiency.

Bitcoin, meanwhile, reacquaints money with a long-lost friend – low time preference. In the absence of supply dilution, everyone's share of money is guaranteed to remain constant in the context of the overall supply, creating an incentive to save it and cultivate better judgment in its deployment. Bitcoin's fixed limit prompts competition among market participants seeking to acquire coins, assuring that they are earned or exchanged for commensurate value, and that their basis for costliness is maintained. Additionally, competition ensures that prices are both quick to adjust and evident in the economy at large, leading to the efficient allocation of resources. The resulting reduction in waste begets lower prices, which stimulates economic growth by increasing the purchasing power of money – growing Bitcoin's value.

4.4.1 CALCULATED RISK: LIQUIDITY TRAP

"The habit of saving is itself an education; it fosters every virtue, teaches self-denial, cultivates a sense of order, trains to forethought, and so broadens the mind."

T. T. MUNGER, RESEARCH SCIENTIST

As a basis for trade (medium of exchange), pricing scale (unit of account), and savings mechanism (store of value), Bitcoin is a honeypot for value, both in the intellectual and monetary senses of the term. Its principled policies incite debate and court attention from economically inclined minds, its costly production and acquisition establishes a substantive basis for value, and its utility entices pioneers of commerce. This attracts capital and liquidity from investors who are captivated by its capabilities, from savers with a low time preference, and from traders drawn to its volatility. As if to prove this point, Wall Street launched Bitcoin futures markets in December 2017[8] and September 2019,[9] showing how even the largest moneyed interests cannot resist its appeal.

More often than not, this appeal is discussed in regard to its investment thesis and, therefore, its potential future value. All investable assets, money and currencies included, are valued based on their perceived risks and rewards. When investing in the pursuit of wealth, it is impossible to completely eliminate risk or guarantee reward, but it is practical to manage them. As such, every investor must strategically evaluate all risks in order to minimize losses and maximize gains.

Bitcoin, as its own new monetary system and asset class, offers an unparalleled risk and reward profile. The key to understanding the opportunity it represents requires putting risk in context.

4.4.2 CALCULATED RISK: EXPECT THE UNEXPECTED

"People think I got into bitcoin because I have a high risk tolerance ... actually I got in because I have a low risk tolerance for worst case scenarios."

JILL CARLSON, CO-FOUNDER OF
OPEN MONEY INITIATIVE

Generally speaking, there are two major risk categories to consider when investing in anything – unsystematic and systematic risk. Unsystematic risks are specific to a particular company, industry, or asset class, with narrow impacts typically associated with factors of productivity, such as land, labor, and physical and intellectual capital. Systematic risk, also known as "market risk," is more comprehensive, with global implications resulting from macro-economic forces such as inflation, interest rates, exchange rates, taxes, or political and social instabilities.

To combat unsystematic risks, many investment funds and wealth managers embrace the mantra of not putting all your eggs in one basket, diversifying portfolios by mixing a variety of asset types across different industries and geographies. This allows smaller and confined risk events negatively affecting one investment to be offset by others that react differently to those same events, or that experience unrelated positive effects.

Guarding against systematic risk is more difficult. Due to the dependency of most financial assets on existing monetary infrastructure, there are fewer opportunities to hedge against it. Historically, gold had a strong track record as just such a hedge, but Bitcoin might have a stronger case. Both are monetary mediums with sound qualities, whose value and utility are not dependent on other financial systems, but only Bitcoin is provably scarce, easy to verify, and globally transferrable at the turn of a digital key.

4.5 Divestment Advice

> *"Bitcoin is not an investment. Bitcoin is a divestment from an unchecked economic system run amok due to decades of easy money printing. It is a hedge against systematic risk."*
>
> Melik Manukyan, Bitcoin Developer

Selecting and constructing an appropriate investment portfolio in pursuit of any desired financial goal is a matter of circumstance and outlook. Prior to making any investment decisions, it is important to have an understanding of your current and future financial needs, the availability of emergency funds, economic and social trends, and tolerance for volatility and loss, in addition to a myriad of other factors.

In the backdrop of an economy whose central banks have clearly demonstrated that their only solution to any forthcoming systemic difficulties is unabashed currency devaluation, and whose governments' only response is more inequitable fiscal largesse, there is a very reasonable case for insuring against fiat fallibility. As its own new asset class and alternative money, Bitcoin can fulfill this role. It improves portfolio diversification, reducing unsystematic risk, and as the sound centerpiece of its own economy that functions irrespective of the legacy system, it is also a hedge against systematic risk.

As a monetary phenomenon with a unique risk profile that is secured by its own independent network, Bitcoin can accurately measure prices, withstand the rigors of time, foster economic efficiencies, and be a magnet for value. Designed to restore the productive capacity of money, it can absorb any and all value that fiat currencies forgo, offering a considerable opportunity for growth today and into the future. As such, investors may be well served to explore its potential, and consider the possible benefits of strategically incorporating Bitcoin into their portfolios.

CHAPTER 5
INNOVATION

5.1.1 EVOLUTION: TRUST > PROOF

"Pay no attention to that man behind the curtain!"

L. FRANK BAUM, *THE WIZARD OF OZ*

Fiat money was once an innovation, which at times made improvements to the age-old challenges of exchanging, dividing, and storing value. However, it is burdened with fatal flaws. It is governed by central authorities that lack a sound basis for trust and whose future policies are uncertain.

Over centuries, fiat currencies have been shaped by the wills and whims of those who ascended into the positions of power entrusted to manage monetary affairs. Susceptible to the blowing winds of social expectations, central banks regularly adjust course hoping to convince markets that each new imposition of monetary policy can guide an economy to prosperity. These authorities must persuade markets of their trustworthiness because, behind the curtain, they have no basis for it. It should therefore come as no surprise that central banks do not treat trust as a two-way street, and never willingly reciprocate the market's faith in them by committing to a predictable policy for any extended timeline.

As with anything though, the effectiveness and confidence in those functions can be superseded by evolutionary or revolutionary creations. Bitcoin's policy is the only one fiat has not and, by all appearances, will not put to the test. By committing to a stable, long-term, and, in Bitcoin's case, systematically enforceable monetary policy, it has rendered obsolete the trust assigned to central banks to morally mold money.

5.1.2 REVOLUTION: PROOF > TRUST

"Don't Trust. Verify."

Bitcoin is a revolutionary advance in money. It tears down the primitive barriers preventing us from freely exchanging, measuring, and securely storing value on our own terms. Its trust-minimizing breakthrough reduces our dependence on rent-seeking middlemen, or "intermediaries," to safeguard funds and process payments, and it also reduces their ability to censor the transmission of our proprietary data. With no need for permission from any financial institution, anyone can independently complete a transaction with their own digital signature – their "private key" – and everyone can verify its existence on the network's public ledger.

As a promising communications technology, Bitcoin's arrival may one day prove to be as significant as the printing press or the Internet. By upending our relationship with trust, it redefines the fundamental premise of money, and while it was designed primarily for that purpose, it is also fueling change relating to commerce, data, and governance.

Bitcoin has established new intellectual common ground in the realms of money, cryptography, computer science, engineering, economics, game theory, psychology, sociology, law, and more. It is a paradigm shift for the concepts of property rights, trust, and cooperation. The full implications of its advent, while hotly debated, discussed, and researched, will not truly be understood for many years, if not decades, much like the Internet.

Trust-Based System   Proof-Based System

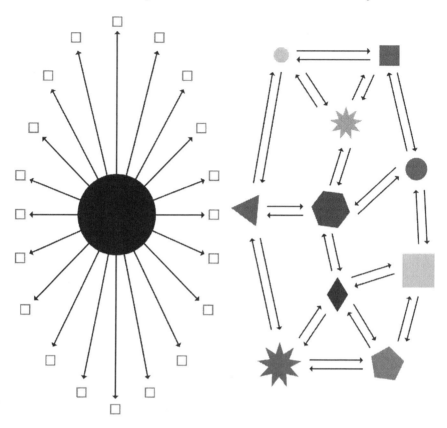

◀ **Trust-Based System:** A central authority dictates the issuance of data and/or value, regardless of its validity. Communication channels are monopolized by the central authority, which arbitrarily determines the rules governing its use.

▶ **Proof-Based System:** Network users cooperate to distribute data and/or value, confirming its validity with multiple sources. Communication channels are accessible to all users, who mutually enforce an agreeable set of rules.

5.2 THE SMART MONEY

"The design supports a tremendous variety of possible trans-action types ... Escrow transactions, bonded contracts, third party arbitration, multi-party signature, etc. If Bitcoin catches on ... these are things we'll want to explore in the future."

SATOSHI NAKAMOTO, CREATOR OF BITCOIN

Traditionally, money has been personified by inanimate objects such as metal coins and paper notes. Regardless of physical form, their standalone utility was limited to direct ownership transference via face-to-face exchange. To administer any further utility, a trusted third party, such as a bank, has typically been required.

Bitcoin, because it is programmable, can be animated to fulfill many useful fiduciary functions in ways other monies cannot, and without the need to trust an intermediary. For instance, banks typically offer joint accounts, which can stipulate that multiple owners of an account must sign to withdraw money. In this example, the bank is the third party that is being trusted to verify the requisite signatures. With Bitcoin, coins can be held in multi-signature addresses, which allow for similar stipulations to be incorporated directly into money, removing the need for third party oversight.

Through the use of built-in functions such as hashlocks and timelocks, Bitcoin can execute a number of other conditional tasks that allow coins to be held as collateral, transferred at a specified time or upon achieving a verifiable milestone, provisionally committed for assurance contracts, and more. By combining the security of cryptography and the practicality of software, the framework for a new monetary system emerges, which eliminates the need to entrust money to a bank by making banking as trustworthy as money itself.

5.3.1 BLOCKCHAIN 101: SHARED LEDGER

"We need to come up with use cases for this technology that drive clear benefits for individuals and institutions – these are our customers. Too often we see Bitcoin and blockchain technologies as solutions in search of a problem."

ABIGAIL JOHNSON, CEO OF FIDELITY INVESTMENTS

One of the innovations upon which Bitcoin was built has spawned an entirely new class of software-based technology. Originally referred to by Satoshi as the "timechain" in an early version of the software, this technology is known today as "blockchain."

A blockchain is a shared ledger – a shared database – that allows multiple users to inscribe transactions. Users append transactions, which are just bits and bytes of data, that get batched into groups known as blocks before being time-stamped, verified by nodes, and bonded together, forming a digital chain. For reference, a node is a computer connected to the network that verifies blocks, and a "full node" goes a step further, saving the complete blockchain – the history of all valid transactions.

As a committed ledger of record, blockchain can dutifully underpin a credible monetary system if it standardizes widely known and agreeable protocols (i.e. predetermined issuance schedule and fixed limit of 21 million coins) that are strictly enforced by consensus (i.e. proof-of-work to prevent partisan modifications).

5.3.2 BLOCKCHAIN 101: IMMUTABLE DATA

"The more people you have to ask for permission, the more dangerous a project gets."

ALAIN DE BOTTON, PHILOSOPHER & AUTHOR

In recent years, blockchain has become a familiar term in business and technology circles, but its meaning and value proposition have been somewhat blurred.

Blockchains can effectively be divided into two types – public and private. Public blockchains, like the Bitcoin chain, have no restrictions on the use of their software and network. On the other hand, private blockchains are intended only for select participants, and permission is required from central authorities in order to gain access. They could be likened to cloud-based databases that, similar to Google Docs, selectively permit multiple users to access, contribute to, and edit a shared document.

A private blockchain typically does not issue any monetary unit, and therefore has no monetary utility or value. This does not preclude such a blockchain from being useful for creating organizational efficiencies, but it can only do so within the walled gardens of its network, and only if implemented impartially. To maintain impartiality, all recorded data must be immutable, meaning that it cannot be altered. If any central authorities retain the ability to overwrite previously recorded transactions, or if the complete dataset cannot be independently verified by any participant, that would negate the point of having the network come to consensus. In the absence of security measures (i.e. mining) to avoid tampering, the purpose of having a blockchain record – a complete, permanent, and sequential dataset – is moot.

Blockchain: An Immutable Ledger Secured by Consensus

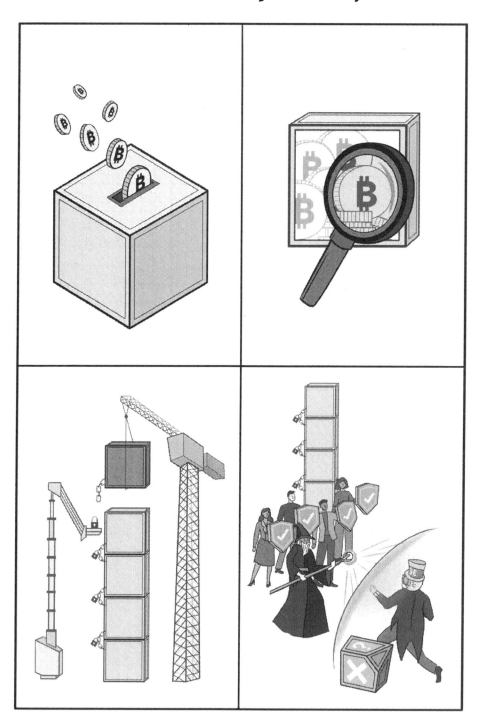

5.3.3 BLOCKCHAIN 101: DESIGN DRIVEN

"Gradually, decentralized trust will be accepted as a new and effective trust model. We have seen this evolution of understanding before – on the Internet."

ANDREAS ANTONOPOLOUS, BITCOIN
ADVOCATE & AUTHOR

Blockchain has a long list of touted properties, but the crux of the technology comes down to removing intermediaries, minimizing the need to trust others, especially to carry out the exchange of valuable proprietary data. By reducing the need to trust intermediaries, users are empowered to secure data (i.e. manage coins) on their own terms.

For a public blockchain to be trusted in lieu of intermediaries, its network must be resilient. For a network to be resilient, security providers (i.e. miners), ledger validators (i.e. nodes), and feature designers (i.e. developers) should be aligned in their concern for the network's continued utility, vitality, and value, which can only be achieved through consistent, just, and inclusive governance (the topic of governance will be explored further in Chapter 9).

To strike this balance, and as a matter of principle, all stakeholders should be fairly compensated for their efforts. By sensibly awarding a native monetary unit to embody the system's value, block rewards act as blockchain's capstone, unifying the interests of all concerned parties involved in self-governing the creation, validation, and security of its proprietary data.

It is crucially important that block rewards be designed to create a positive feedback loop for value and trust. Their economics and utility must equitably empower and incentivize users to achieve the common goal of sustaining the network, especially since it exists for their mutual benefit. This is blockchain's most potent utility – the reinforcement of public collaboration.

5.3.4 BLOCKCHAIN 101: NETWORK EFFECTS

> *"It is no wonder that eight years after its invention, block-chain technology has not yet managed to break through in a successful, ready-for-market commercial application other than the one for which it was specifically designed: Bitcoin."*
>
> SAIFEDEAN AMMOUS, *THE BITCOIN STANDARD*

If blockchain is best understood as a tool for public collaboration, and if block rewards are the method by which participants are enticed to discover, expand, and utilize the network's value, and if that value can be freely transferred, secured, and accounted for in a trust-minimized environment, then a well-designed blockchain invariably exhibits the attributes and functions of money. Since there is no other embodiment of value that can be both fully functional and fully verifiable as a purely digital entity, money necessarily rises to the fore as blockchain's most compelling use.

Many public blockchains such as Litecoin, Zcash, and Ethereum (more to come on these in Chapter 8) are attempting to funnel trust and value into their networks through the creative adaptation of blockchain principles, effectively testing the limits of its functionality, but none are more proficient than Bitcoin. Its value has grown faster than any other asset since its inception,[10] and it is the most liquid of all blockchains. More importantly though, it is by far the costliest. Costliness is a crucial quality of money because it ensures that money cannot be taken for granted. Whether measured by its exchange price in financial markets or the resource requirements of mining, Bitcoin is perpetually costly to procure.

The competitive forces propelling Bitcoin's costs continuously earn the trust of users by maintaining the consistency of its monetary protocols, the immutability of its ledger, the freedom to participate without permission, and the robustness of its security.[11] Accordingly, Bitcoin seems to be emerging as exemplary money in part because it is an exemplary blockchain.

CHAPTER 6

RESILIENCE

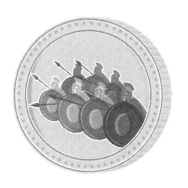

6.1 AN UNSTOPPABLE FORCE

"Bitcoin is underpinned by math and cryptography. Like gravity, it works whether you like it or not."

CAMERON WINKLEVOSS, VENTURE CAPITALIST

One of the reasons Bitcoin is so impressive is that it's been continuously broadcasting truthful copies of and updates to its ledger of transactions 24 hours a day, 7 days a week, and 365 days a year, ever since the Genesis block. The network does not stop, and the network does not lie. It is extremely difficult to censor anyone from performing a transaction, and everyone can verify the existence of a transaction. The full ledger is considered immutable because data cannot be reversed, altered, or deleted. Once a transaction is sent, it is permanent.

This finality of transactions is intentional. It removes the role of intermediaries that act as both custodians and arbiters of money. Although finality deprives users of the convenience of contacting an administrator to reverse mistakes, there are savings from this subtraction. The ability to dispute transactions can lead to carelessness in transaction execution, which can be expensive to administer and then remedy, and it also leaves the door open for influential third parties such as governments to impose restrictions on how and when money is used.

Bitcoin fixes this by being mercilessly egalitarian. It demands accountability from users in order to minimize the potential for interference from adversarial third parties. To those who place a high value on having total control over their money, this cost is decidedly worth its price.

6.2 Teamwork Makes the Dream Work

"If you want to go fast, go alone. If you want to go far, go together."

African Proverb

According to Metcalfe's law,[12] the effect of a communications network is proportional to the square of its number of connected users. To illustrate this point, consider the fax machine. A single machine, with nowhere to send documents and no peers to receive them from, is useless. However, when connected to others, its utility increases with each additional machine it can interact with. This also applies to social networks. The more users one has, the more valuable it becomes to its community. The effectiveness of Bitcoin could be viewed similarly. When Satoshi first launched Bitcoin, it was a network of one, and was therefore useless. A few days after launch, Hal Finney joined the network and received the first ever transaction from Satoshi – 10 bitcoins on January 12, 2009 – igniting its utility.

Today Bitcoin has connected users all over the world working together to reinforce its effectiveness. The network is considered "decentralized" because no user has absolute authority over any aspect of it, and all users bear some responsibility for its maintenance. Also, because any user can maintain a copy of the software and chain history, it is considered "distributed." With no focal point to attack, these diffusions reduce the network's potential vulnerabilities.

Bitcoin's users, comprised of miners, node operators, developers, and coin owners, cooperate with one another because they value the network's utility. This collaboration is precisely the reason that Bitcoin is likely to endure over time, because the combined efforts of users are greater than the sum of their parts.

Network Effects of Metcalfe's Law

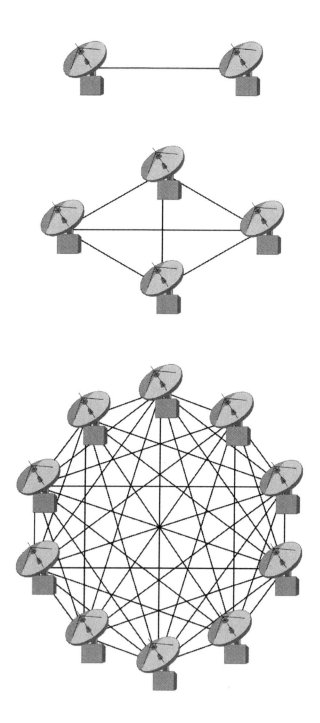

6.3 An Immovable Object

"In matters of style, swim with the current; in matters of principle, stand like a rock."

THOMAS JEFFERSON, 3RD PRESIDENT
OF THE UNITED STATES

Throughout its history, there have been several attempts to manipulate Bitcoin, but none have been successful. Bitcoin has proven that it can withstand attacks from governments, institutions, and even its own miners. Unintentional or geographically contained events such as power and Internet outages are temporary and limited.

In 2017, it even survived a major conflict among some of its most ardent supporters. During that episode, a group of influential figureheads, currency exchanges, entrepreneurs, and miners lobbied for a controversial protocol change to increase the block size from 1 megabyte to 8 megabytes. This was intended to increase Bitcoin's transaction capacity, but the added data would have overly burdened common computers and Internet connections, negatively impacting decentralization. When implementation was attempted, the proposal was firmly rejected by Bitcoin's quiet, disperse, and loyal bookkeepers – its nodes – which refused to run that proposed version of the software.

A similarly powerful consortium would have had their way in just about any other industry, but due to the pivotal role that nodes play in decentralizing authority, they swiftly dismissed this scheme simply by running the same software they always run.

This is a fitting example of the operational fortitude and integrity of Bitcoin. As concerned citizens, nodes continually cast votes that determine consensus, confirming the valid state of the blockchain and its rules of engagement. This helps to ensure that its ledger remains immutable and its agreed upon rules are never broken.

6.4 HARDER, BETTER, FASTER, STRONGER

"Antifragility is beyond resilience or robustness. The resilient resists shocks and stays the same; the antifragile gets better."

NASSIM NICHOLAS TALEB, AUTHOR,
SCHOLAR & STATISTICIAN

Not only is Bitcoin extremely difficult to manipulate, but its community of developers and supporters regularly contribute to its evolution, improving its strengths and shielding its weaknesses. Some recent and noteworthy developments include:

- Blockstream launching a satellite to broadcast Bitcoin's ledger data from space, making it accessible to the majority of the world, regardless of Internet connectivity;
- Mesh network devices, such as goTenna, which can relay transactions in the absence of cell, Wi-Fi, or satellite service;
- Open-source software applications such as BTCPay Server, which allows anyone to become a payment processor; and
- There has even been a recorded instance of a transaction being broadcast via radio waves.

These examples highlight how Bitcoin developers and contributors are not only focused on improving the Bitcoin software itself, but are making concerted efforts to ensure that it can function adequately in worst-case scenarios by surrounding it with a suite of complimentary products and services. Each new method for transacting with and verifying Bitcoin enhances the network's resilience, which grows more formidable each day, bolstering prospects for its long-term autonomy and durability.

CHAPTER 7
SCARCITY

7.1 LIMITED EDITION

"Nothing creates cool like scarcity."

NEIL BLUMENTHAL, CO-FOUNDER OF WARBY PARKER

Scarcity simply means being in short supply. A thing is not necessarily valuable just because its quantity is finite, but value almost always has roots in such limitations. Nothing that is abundant or can easily be procured maintains value, and, intuitively, people tend to want that which is difficult to obtain, making scarcity a value-adding premium. This principle is well established in both social psychology and economics.

Popular culture perfectly demonstrates this concept. It is common for limited edition products to command a financial premium due in large part to their low supplies. For example, an article of clothing from a coveted brand, like Supreme, can command much higher prices than other products of similar quality and style due to little else besides its label, which famously only releases products in strictly limited quantities.

Some fundamental questions arise from this example. Why is the brand coveted? What makes it desirable and, as a result, valuable? The answer is that rare things are in one way or another differentiated by some defining characteristics. In the art or fashion industries, those may include an item's aesthetic beauty, fine craftsmanship, original design, nostalgic sentiment, or even mystique – like that of the pseudonymous artist Banksy – along with a million other factors that tug at human interests. To attract value, scarce items always exhibit traits that stand out as being special.

7.2 $€¥£: A Sea of Fiat

"There's plenty of money out there. They print more every day. But this ticket, there's only five of them in the whole world, and that's all there's ever going to be. Only a dummy would give this up for something as common as money. Are you a dummy?"

ROALD DAHL, *CHARLIE & THE CHOCOLATE FACTORY*

Generally speaking, money has its own set of inherent value drivers. As mentioned in Chapter 3, some of these include the creditworthiness of the issuer, as well as demand and supply, which we shall review here. Not previously mentioned was the utility of money, meaning the scope of its functionality, which will come into focus later in this chapter.

Coins and notes come in various sizes, materials, and designs, but aesthetics are essentially unrelated to monetary value. While it may be convenient to think that the value of fiat currencies is correlated to economic output, reality is more nuanced. For example, assuming all else is equal, if frugal-minded Switzerland was believed to be more likely to repay its loans than debt-ridden Japan, then on that basis alone Switzerland may be perceived as more creditworthy, and the Swiss Franc therefore more valuable, than the Japanese Yen. However, if amicable Japan brokered deals with other nations to use the Yen for international trade settlement, but neutral Switzerland forged no agreements for the Franc, then Japan's currency would be in higher demand, and therefore more valuable on that basis.

No matter the demand or creditworthiness of a currency, supply is the ultimate arbiter of value. In fiat monetary systems, a tsunami of additional supply could strike at any moment, ravaging any other built-up value. With no assured ceiling on the amount of currency that can be printed, there is no floor preventing fiat currency's value from sinking to zero.

7.3 SETTING A PRECEDENT

"Bitcoin is a remarkable cryptographic achievement and the ability to create something that is not duplicable in the digital world has enormous value."

ERIC SCHMIDT, FORMER CEO & CHAIRMAN OF GOOGLE

Harder monies stand on firmer footing. Gold was once very attractive as money because it is the scarcest of earth's natural resources, its most malleable element, and also aesthetically pleasing. To this day, explorers scour the world's surfaces for hints of its existence below their feet, while others search the stars,[13] with dreams of mining the mineral riches of asteroids in the cosmos. And yet, as the former champion of scarce money, we cannot verify any firm limit for the global – or universal – gold supply.

Bitcoin challenges gold in this regard because its scarcity is known to have an absolute limit. In economic terms, it has a perfectly inelastic supply. As mentioned in Chapter 2, Bitcoin was founded on the promise that there would only ever be 21 million bitcoins, and not a sat more. Satoshi sealed this promise by presciently defining Bitcoin as the chain with the most proof-of-work. Known as "Nakamoto Consensus," this definition asserts that the totality of evidence accumulated on its chain, settled through the costly rigors of mining and verified by nodes, proves the singularity of its ledger. In other words, in existential fashion, Bitcoin exists to prove its own scarcity.

This systematic commitment to transparently affirming its own credibility is truly one of a kind, and it ensures that all of Bitcoin's attributed value must fit within the strict confines of its 21 million coins.

7.4 Pushing Limits

"You have given them an ideal to aspire to, embodied their highest aspirations. They will race, and stumble, and fall and crawl ... and curse ... and finally ... They will join you in the sun, Kal-El ... In time you will help them accomplish wonders."

Grant Morrison, *All-Star Superman*, Vol. 2

Unlike state sponsored money, Bitcoin's creditworthiness can only be measured based on its ability to stick to its foundational promise of a fixed supply (so far so good) since it has no capacity to borrow. With no governing body soliciting demand through trade agreements, what is it then, aside from its fixed supply, that makes Bitcoin so special that we should find it worthwhile? As with other discoveries and inventions, demand for Bitcoin is a function of its utility – its usefulness.

Bitcoin exhibits a myriad of abilities previously unknown to money, inviting value to its scarce supply in ways that other monies can only dream of. Consider the hypotheses below.

- Has there ever been money that can fulfill the fiduciary duties of a bank without having to trust a banker? *No, but Bitcoin does because it's programmable.*
- Has money ever moved as freely as radio waves through thin air? *No, but Bitcoin does because it's censorship resistant.*
- Has the security of a bank vault ever been as convenient as e-mail? *No, but Bitcoin is because it's seizure resistant.*
- Have financial regulations ever afforded users the discretion of cash? *No, but Bitcoin does because it's pseudonymous, and participation does not require permission.*

Bitcoin's Utility-Value Feedback Loop

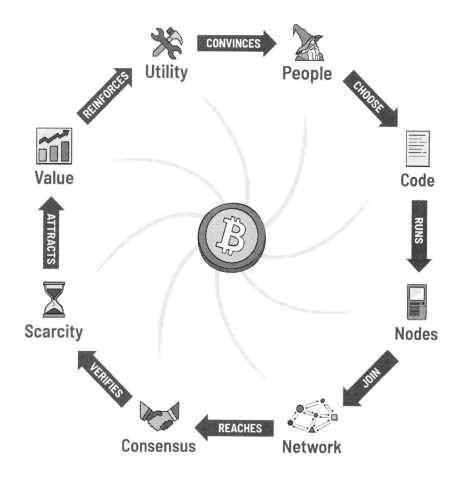

The Importance of Utility: Bitcoin is scarce not only because it has a fixed supply, but also because it is unusually useful. This functionality plays a key role in the positive feedback loop for its value. Should an individual become captivated by any one of its uses or characteristics, it is more likely than not that they will be drawn to others as well. This is the force of "Bitcoin's Gravity," as described by Gigi in a blog post of the same name. The model above was adapted from the "Idea-Value Feedback Loop" presented in that same post.

Source: https://dergigi.com/2019/05/01/bitcoins-gravity/

7.5 Making a Statement

"Symbolism erects a façade of respectability to hide the indecency of dreams."

Mason Cooley, Aphorist & Professor Emeritus

The standard symbol for US dollars is "$." It is also expressed as an abbreviation, using the ticker "USD." Other monies have similar notations, and as a player in that same sandbox, so too does Bitcoin. It is usually abbreviated as "BTC," and symbolized as "₿." Needless to say, Bitcoin's standing as money is not a result of these symbols, but they do reinforce it. Similarly, Bitcoin's brand identity is supported by its fixed limit of 21 million coins. Almost anyone who knows about Bitcoin is familiar with this aspect of it because it is distinctive, memorable, and straightforward.

In practice, Bitcoin's status as compelling money is backed by a number of reflexive feedback loops, which court attention, uphold its reputation, and bolster its value. To wit, as the first successful implementation of electronic money (see Chapter 2) that is a bastion of soundness (see Chapter 3), highly economical (see Chapter 4), trust-minimized (see Chapter 5), reliable (see Chapter 6), limited (this chapter), preferable (see Chapter 8), equitable (see Chapter 9), independent (see Chapter 10), and timely (see Chapter 12), Bitcoin breathes rarefied air. Almost everything about it is alluring and advantageous.

This is especially impressive given that Bitcoin is a community-driven effort with no institutional sponsor. No amount of national or corporate influence could have imbued the stature that Bitcoin has freely attained. Its prominence is a direct result of its singular utility, which is not only uncommon, but also ideal for a monetary system.

7.6 NO SECOND CHANCE FOR FIRST IMPRESSIONS

"So I guess I'm one of a kind in a full house."

J. IVY, "NEVER LET ME DOWN" AS
PRESENTED ON HBO DEF POETRY

In recent years, Nassim Nicholas Taleb popularized a theory called the "Lindy effect,"[14] which suggests that the longer a technological or conceptual phenomenon exists, the longer it can be expected to exist. Bitcoin, as if by gravitational pull, draws in open-minded researchers, developers, engineers, entrepreneurs, investors, and more to partner in and benefit from upholding its network and ideology. As a single, unifying, and resilient system, Bitcoin typifies this theory, leaving little doubt that it will hold true for a long time to come.

Going forward, if Bitcoin continues cementing itself into minds and marketplaces, then one day it may very well become more supremely coveted than any other embodiment of scarcity known below the ground, beyond the stars, or throughout cyberspace.

Curiously, few understand the degree to which any attempt at creating a similar system necessarily lives in Bitcoin's shadow. An idea and instrument as resounding as Bitcoin is unlikely to be unseated by any imitator, no matter how flattering. Any successive system advantaged by Bitcoin's example must not only match its efficacy on all fronts, but surpass it, and the likelihood of that happening is scarce indeed.

CHAPTER 8
COMPETITION

8.1 A NEW FRONTIER

"We ask only that we be permitted to compete on an even basis, and if we are not worthy, then the competition shall, per se, eliminate us."

JACKIE ROBINSON, HUMANITARIAN, FIRST PROFESSIONAL
AFRICAN-AMERICAN BASEBALL PLAYER

Like the taxi industry before ride-sharing, fiat money was for decades a deeply entrenched monopoly, with no impetus for meaningful improvement, and no expectation of any imminent or existential threat. It operated with impunity.

That state of affairs was permanently changed with the arrival of Bitcoin. Its launch marked the opening salvo of a new arms race to reimagine money for the 21st century and beyond. Like the Space Race before it, where Cold War foes the United States and the Soviet Union competed to be the first to achieve spaceflight, the race for monetary supremacy marks a defining moment in history. It has galvanized institutions and individuals, the vast majority of whom had previously treated the conceptual foundations of money as an afterthought, into scrutinizing its purpose and performance.

Moving forward, the medium that best embodies the desired characteristics of money, as demanded by global markets in the wake of this heightened interest, will likely accrue the most value into the extended future.

The remainder of this chapter is dedicated to directly comparing Bitcoin against the other monetary mediums with which it competes for that treasured mindshare and value.

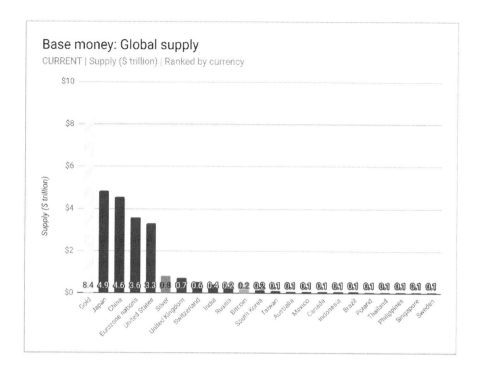

Base money: Global supply

CURRENT | Supply ($ trillion) | Ranked by currency

Supply ($ trillion)

8.4 4.9 4.6 3.6 3.3 0.8 0.7 0.6 0.4 0.2 0.2 0.2 0.1 0.1 0.1 0.1 0.1 0.1 0.1 0.1 0.1 0.1 0.1

Gold · Japan · China · Eurozone nations · United States · Silver · United Kingdom · Switzerland · India · Russia · Bitcoin · South Korea · Taiwan · Australia · Mexico · Canada · Indonesia · Brazil · Poland · Thailand · Philippines · Singapore · Sweden

Global Base Money Comparison: Charting the value of the top 20 global currencies, as well as gold, silver, and Bitcoin. Here, base money is defined as physical currency in circulation plus commercial bank reserves, because it is the final form of money – irredeemable for anything else – and is representative of Bitcoin's direct competition. Data has been sourced from various central bank balance sheets. The complete dataset and methodology can be found at: https://cryptovoices.com/basemoney

8.2 BITCOIN VERSUS FIAT

"The history of fiat money is little more than a register of monetary follies and inflations. Our present age merely affords another entry into this dismal register."

HANS F. SENNHOLZ, AUSTRIAN ECONOMIST

Fiat is the grease that keeps the wheels of the global economy spinning. Whether those wheels spin fast or slow, forwards or backwards, in slippery mud or on firm road is up for debate. In many respects, the economics and social payoffs of fiat leaves much to be desired of a monetary system, especially when compared to Bitcoin.

Most fiat currencies in the world today have been around for several decades or, in some select cases, over a century. However, they all have failed ancestors dating back over a millennium. From the Jiaozi of the Chinese Song Dynasty in the 10th century to the Papiermark of the German Weimar Republic in the 20th century, time has never been kind to fiat money. Nonetheless, currencies today continue to be created at will and at no cost, mirroring the events that led to the demise of their predecessors.

Today, the world's fiat currencies are cumulatively valued at approximately $20 trillion USD. Bitcoin, by comparison, which in January 2020 turned 11 years old, is worth less than $0.2 trillion USD at an assumed price of $10,000 per coin. That is nearly 1% of the value of all fiat currency. The gap between those values is only partially indicative of the addressable market for Bitcoin should it continue to develop and improve into decidedly better money.

8.3 BITCOIN VERSUS GOLD

"The desire of gold is not for gold. It is for the means of freedom and benefit."

RALPH WALDO EMERSON, WRITER & PHILOSOPHER

As the previous backbone of the world's monetary system, in addition to being a scarce and beautiful asset, gold retains a significant amount of value and is a globally recognized symbol of wealth. Today, all the known gold in the world is estimated to be valued at over $8 trillion USD.

As a monetary medium, gold's role has recently skewed primarily towards being a store of value, since it no longer forms the basis of exchange, and is almost never used as a unit of account. Even if it was used for trade, as an analog yellow metal it lacks product-market fit in an increasingly digital world where physical cash is becoming less prevalent. In that regard, it would face stiff competition from the likes of Bitcoin, which is much easier to store, transport, divide, verify, and transact with.

Looking forward, gold is unlikely to reclaim its standing as the go-to monetary medium because it has largely been consolidated into bank vaults, from which it is unlikely to be redistributed via commerce. The only route for gold to regain monetary relevance would be if it was re-collateralized by central banks to support the value of their currencies. However, the centrally controlled nature of large global gold supplies would require that we trust central banks to accurately account for them. Given how that same trust was broken mere decades ago, we would be foolish to make that same mistake again.

8.4 BITCOIN VERSUS CRYPTO

"If you think cryptography is the answer to your problem, then you don't know what your problem is."

PETER G. NEUMANN, COMPUTER SCIENTIST

"Crypto" is short for cryptography, but these days the term is more commonly known as a reference to the financial markets of blockchain-based digital assets. These are also sometimes referred to as "cryptocurrencies" or "cryptoassets."

There's a wide array of initiatives in crypto, and their potential applications are limited only by the imaginations of their developers. Some of the more well-known examples include Litecoin,[15] which aspired to be the silver to Bitcoin's digital gold, and sometimes moonlights as a testnet for Bitcoin. There is Zcash,[16] an enigmatic, privacy-focused currency that broadcasted its launch ceremony live on the Internet, and allots 20% of coin issuance to its founders. There is also Ethereum,[17] which initially offered its coins as digital gas for fueling a world computer, and presently fuels a complex economy of digital tokens.

Within the broader crypto landscape, some projects are clever and well intentioned, some are outright scams, and some are just electronic Rube Goldberg machines[18] – overly touted and complicated systems that provide little real value.

Generally speaking, crypto introduces users to elements of decentralized networks, driving speculative interest, but their incentive mechanisms may be suspect, susceptible to arbitrary modification, or, worse, wholly fail to align the interests of all stakeholders. Whether or not any crypto can ultimately challenge Bitcoin's market dominance remains to be seen, but unless proven otherwise, Bitcoin is the *de facto* monetary standard and preferred reserve asset of the global crypto economy.

8.5 BITCOIN VERSUS FORKS

"Any successful replacement of the Bitcoin blockchain will forever undermine the credibility of any successor. How is an investor to know that it won't happen again?"

HAL FINNEY, CYPHERPUNK, COMPUTER
SCIENTIST, BITCOIN PIONEER

Bitcoin developers diligently push out protocol upgrades to modify network rules and features, but this process tends to occur slowly and methodically to ensure mutual benefit for all users, and also to avoid mistakes that might threaten the integrity of the network. If a change is agreeable and compatible with the original chain, it is known as a "soft fork." If a change is agreeable and incompatible, something Bitcoin avoids in order to maintain the singularity of its chain, it is called a "hard fork." If a change is both disagreeable and incompatible, it can cause the blockchain to split into multiple chains. This is known as a "contentious hard fork."

Contentious hard forks are lobbied for by a subset of users who represent narrow interests. They seek to dictate terms of the network without reaching consensus by copying the software and re-launching it, detached from the original chain, with modified protocols. This conduct circumvents the previously agreed upon rules, undermining both the systemic properties upholding Bitcoin's integrity and the entire value proposition of protocol-driven collaboration. Like any knockoff item, these forks are inexpensive to produce, inauthentic, and they may deceive unsuspecting buyers.

Although several forks exist today, they can only claim to be tall because they stand on the shoulders of a giant. Only the chain originally envisioned and launched by Satoshi – BTC, the longest chain – has the most proof-of-work and maintains a direct link to the Genesis block, thereby preserving its credibility as a monetary phenomenon.

8.6 BITCOIN VERSUS STABLECOINS

"Meet the new boss. Same as the old boss."

PETE TOWNSEND, "WON'T GET FOOLED AGAIN"

Large institutions have signaled their intent to issue their own digital currencies. The World Economic Forum even launched a framework for their deployment,[19] validating the concept of distributed networks as practical value transfer mechanisms. The most prominent examples of these today are Facebook's Libra project[20] and China's Digital Currency Electronic Payment (DCEP) project,[21] although several other global central banks are also openly contemplating similar schemes.

All of these projects share two important commonalities. First, in monetary terms they are new digital representations of the same old fiat currencies. They treat a symptom of financial woes, namely payment convenience, without addressing the root problems caused by reckless monetary policies and trusted third parties. Second, from a technological standpoint, their designs are akin to private blockchains, which in all likelihood will be run by central authorities that retain censorship privileges. All told, this concept is like a paint job for a car in need of a new engine.

Digital currencies with face values equivalent to whichever fiat currency they represent are known as "stablecoins." They could be likened to digital casino chips because they tend to be most useful under the casino's eye-in-the-sky surveillance apparatus. With this gambit, the issuing authority has no need for favored gaming odds. Instead, it can be expected that they will extract their pound of flesh from valuable personal data by monitoring, analyzing, and regulating your transactions.

CHAPTER 9

GOVERNANCE

9.1 FAIR IS RARE

"Magic Mirror on the wall, who is the fairest one of all?"
WALT DISNEY PRODUCTIONS, *SNOW
WHITE & THE SEVEN DWARFS*

Good governance is all about fairness. The best a governing body can hope to achieve is fair opportunity and benefits for its constituents. Of course, nothing that exists in this world is perfectly fair. There are only degrees of fairness. This is an unfortunate and sober truth, because the world is finite and there is only so much of anything to go around. Things seldom originate everywhere, all at once, in quantities that will satisfy the wants of everyone. And even if they did, the principle of scarcity suggests that they would not be valuable or desirable.

Money, like everything else, also exhibits higher or lower degrees of fairness, and for the most part, this results from its governance. What is its monetary policy? How are decisions made? How is the governing body structured? The answers to these questions help inform on the nature of equality afforded to constituents.

Bitcoin's governance is reasonably well balanced. Its operations are fully transparent, and there are no restrictions on participation. The barriers to joining or leaving the network are practically non-existent, and it works on a level playing field, affording all users equal opportunity to earn money and shape policy.

As for fiat currency, its scales are tilted. It is managed entirely behind closed doors, and its prohibitive use is insisted upon by law, since governments are wholly dependent on its continued use to fund their bloated administration. The inherent unfairness of its governance rests in the authority to create money, which is a central bank monopoly, and to distribute money, which is a commercial bank oligopoly.

9.2.1 TILTED: DEBT FROM THIN AIR

"This unique attribute of the banking business was discovered many centuries ago ... bankers discovered that they could make loans merely by giving their promises to pay ... In this way, banks began to create money."

FEDERAL RESERVE BANK OF CHICAGO,
"MODERN MONEY MECHANICS"

Control over fiat monetary policy is a private party, and ordinary people are not invited. Central banks retain the sole, discretionary ability to create currency by making new entries into their own private, unaudited ledger, and also to set the baseline interest rate for lending throughout their subservient banking system.

Once created, central banks deposit new currency with commercial banks, which distribute it through a process called "fractional-reserve banking." This system grants commercial banks a license to create additional money that they do not possess, merely by issuing loans – credits – against existing deposits – debits – without actually withdrawing funds from those deposits. In other words, loans made by banks are not pre-existing funds lent from one account to another, properly balancing credits and debits. Instead, they're unsubstantiated paper promises, conjuring new credit entries from thin air, like pulling a rabbit out of a hat.

This privileged practice, reserved only for banks, is the soil in which the fiat financial system grows its magic money trees. Loans, as the roots of those trees, are a key driver of today's global economy, and since most debts are directly affected by interest rates, which are controlled by central banks, the resulting influence exerted by central banks over the global economy is unjustly magnified.

9.2.2 TILTED: THE EXCLUSIVITY ERR

"Men might as well be imprisoned, as excluded from the means of earning their bread."

JOHN STUART MILL, *ON LIBERTY*

Banks and governments benefit from the "Cantillon Effect," which is the unequal access to new money. This effect suggests that the first recipients of newly created money, by virtue of their proximity to the point of origin, are conveniently positioned to benefit from its creation. For all intents and purposes, spending or investing new currency before it permeates through the economy raises prices for those who are the last to use it. This means that being close to the source of money creation is a distinct advantage, while those who are farthest from it are disadvantaged.

Furthermore, the use of national currencies is enforced by legal tender laws, which for many countries dictate that local fiat must be accepted as a means of payment for debts, public charges, taxes, and dues. This is the antithesis of fair competition and free market principles, since it self-servingly deters the use of alternatives. It also diminishes the conceptual value of money as a public good because money's creation and distribution channels are not actually available to the public.

When it comes down to it, government needs to control money far more than money needs to be controlled by government. This immensely impactful yet oft overlooked source of power affords authorities undue influence over economic activity, permitting central banks and governments to subjugate our livelihoods to their misguided mandates and failing to equitably promote prosperity.

9.3.1 BALANCED: OPPORTUNITY TO SPARE

"The road to long-term monetary stability leads ultimately to the complete abolition of the government monopoly of issuing money and, concomitantly, to the return of the function of supplying money to the free market."

J.T. SALERNO, AMERICAN-AUSTRIAN ECONOMIST

Bitcoin's viability as a monetary alternative was never and is not guaranteed. No status was ever appropriated or conferred, and all trust in its abilities has been and continues to be earned. Its arrival was fair because it had no precedent, was thrust into the public domain in one fell swoop, and was free to spread at the speed of information. The seeds of its distribution were sewn through free markets and human ingenuity. The early Bitcoin users, including Satoshi, expended their own hardware, energy, and time to bootstrap the network with no assurance that their efforts would pay off.

Some may discount the efforts of early adopters, believing them lucky or unfairly advantaged, yet who among us can honestly say they would have actually supported Bitcoin when it was worthless or worth very little? Who among us dismissed the idea when they first heard about it? Who among us would bother working on a project offering no income and no equity, which had no distinguishable strategy to solicit a valuation or provide any return on investment?

In truth, Bitcoin's early contributors were modern-day explorers choosing to risk personal resources in the hopes of discovering something valuable and useful. Some even set up no-strings-attached "faucets," sharing free fractions of bitcoins from block rewards with new users in order to widen its distribution and encourage others to explore its capabilities.

At no point did waving a magic wand or dreaming up credits on a private ledger ever generate any bitcoins. No license can exempt another from participating, nor from playing by the rules, and the system is intentionally left open for any users to share in its risks and benefits. The fairness inherent in this design is strikingly high.

9.3.2 BALANCED: EARN YOUR SHARE

"Because of the extremely high stakes, reinventing a monetary system is a profoundly unpleasant task. It takes irrational zeal and an unwavering commitment to a firm vision of the future."

NIC CARTER, PARTNER AT CASTLE ISLAND VENTURES

During Bitcoin's infancy, software bugs were commonplace, and crude functionality meant that it was cumbersome to successfully manage "private keys" – the literal key to unlocking a wallet's coins. With negligible value, written keys on paper and digital keys on old hard drives or memory sticks were often forgotten, misplaced, or thrown away.

As a result of its various limitations, difficulties, and vulnerabilities, the fruits of many early contributors' labor are likely gone forever. In November 2019, Coin Metrics, a blockchain data and research company, attempted to quantify these losses, estimating that roughly 1.5 million bitcoins have been permanently lost, representing 7% of the total supply.[22]

Over time, as Bitcoin's software and applications have evolved, in part thanks to the trials and tribulations of early users, so too has the ease with which coins can be secured. Improvements have led to the growth of complimentary products and services, which attracts liquidity and exposes prospective users to the network's utility, concurrently distributing coin ownership and growing the network, along with Bitcoin's value.

Though not without its challenges, Bitcoin's emergence has been a free market revelation. Living on the most unrestricted and accessible channel in existence – the Internet – its path has been more honest, fair, and transparent than any other known resource, idea, or currency, which might otherwise have been patented, sequestered, or in some way stymied from uninhibited adoption.

9.4.1 GROUND RULES: CODE IS LAW

"Code is the most significant form of law that humans have ever been exposed to."

PROFESSOR LAWRENCE LESSIG, AUTHOR OF CODE 2.0

On January 1, 2000, New Year's Day of the current millennium, *Harvard Magazine* printed an article called "Code Is Law."[23] In it, law professor Lawrence Lessig explained how every age has its dominant regulatory force, which invariably threatens fairness and freedom in some capacity.

He pointed out that in this burgeoning age of cyberspace, code sets the terms that govern its experience for both the protection of privacy and the censorship of speech, because both can be fully and automatically enforced. Additionally, as code changes, it subsequently determines the ongoing character of cyberspace. He therefore suggests that unless the principles upheld by code are kept in check, it may alter or displace our moral compass.

Since programming is akin to writing digital laws, he goes on to ask how the public could have a role in shaping the governance of cyberspace, and what values it should uphold? In a world relying more and more on code as a materially impactful type of law, he argues that code should be tested and interrogated. In conclusion, he submits that unless we learn how to self-govern and protect our rights in cyberspace, they may go unrepresented and fade away.

Although there are many types of laws and activities that cannot be enforced by code, money, as demonstrated by Bitcoin, is one that absolutely can be.

9.4.2 GROUND RULES: SOCIAL CONTRACT IS MONEY

"Nothing appears more surprising to those who consider human affairs ... than the easiness with which the many are governed by the few."

DAVID HUME, "OF THE FIRST PRINCIPLES OF GOVERNMENT"

Money requires more than binding enforcement though, if it is to be considered fair and credible. It requires the consent of the governed, because at its core, money is a social contract that only functions when it is socially acceptable. Today, the primary reason that fiat serves as the dominant monetary medium, despite its flaws, is because it is the world's "Schelling Point" for money.

In game theory, a Schelling Point is the default position chosen for its natural and obvious prominence. The longstanding institutionalization of fiat currency has led to the widespread expectation and belief that fiat is indeed satisfactory money, especially since it is so widely accepted. This is the social contract that the world has, somewhat unwittingly, agreed to since the dissolution of the gold standard. As a result, we are all socially complicit with the nation state's assertion of authoritarian governance over money, unfair though it may be.

To change the social contract of money, the world must decide on a new Schelling Point. Bitcoin now appears to be the most viable candidate for this, and it is the reason that figurative negotiations are underway in money markets for new contractual terms. Its accountable and transparent policies have started a dialogue that is shifting our preferences for money by setting a higher standard for its equitable creation, distribution, security, utility, value, and governance.

9.4.3 GROUND RULES: SOCIAL CONSENSUS IS THE PEOPLE'S MONEY

"Consensus is the worst form of monetary governance, except for all the others."

JIMMY SONG, BITCOIN EDUCATOR,
DEVELOPER & ENTREPRENEUR

The authoritarian approach of fiat currency leaves much to be desired for the good governance of a monetary system because it is fundamentally biased. Bitcoin, by comparison, is impartial because it is based on code that incorporates elements of both meritocracy and democracy.

Bitcoin is meritocratic because anybody can propose changes or additions to its protocols by publishing a Bitcoin Improvement Proposal (BIP). Subsequently, anyone can evaluate and build upon those ideas. Proposals considered to be the cream of the crop inevitably advance to the fore based on their expected added benefit to Bitcoin. This attracts developers to help build out and test those proposals for wide scale deployment.

Bitcoin could also be considered partly democratic because nodes act as Bitcoin's congress, continually casting votes for their preferred version of the software with each new block that they verify. Once a proposal is fully tested and released, nodes can choose whether or not to run the new version of the software based on their view of its impact. In this way, nodes determine the ongoing state of Bitcoin's laws by updating its code in a principled, representative, and timely fashion.

By incorporating the social contract of money into the resolute laws of code, Bitcoin is inclusive of its stakeholders in soliciting and evaluating ideas for new rules, and also reliant on their active participation in order to implement them. In this way, Bitcoin is socially scalable, and it achieves what could be thought of as social consensus,[24] with its laws written by, agreed to, and enforced by its constituency.

9.5 LEAD BY EXAMPLE

*"Do you truly believe that life is fair, Señor de la Vega?
– No, maestro, but I plan to do everything in my power to
make it so."*

ISABEL ALLENDE, ZORRO

The opposing styles of monetary governance reviewed in this chapter could be summed up as follows: whereas fiat is building walls, Bitcoin is building bridges. The legacy monetary system has established moats to legally insulate and institutionalize its control over zero-cost money creation, distribution, and governance. On the other hand, Bitcoin is costly to produce, its value is open to the public for discovery, its distribution is fulfilled by the collaborative power of free markets, and its governance is represented and enforced by its constituents.

Those who support, transact with, and value Bitcoin do so at their own risk, as has been the case since its inception. Participation in its governance is entirely voluntary, and anyone can opt in or out at any time. No authority insists on its use, and the ability to affect change is justly balanced among its stakeholders. This shrewd and uncompromising decentralization of responsibility is Bitcoin's great equalizer, and, although it may not be perfect, it is no less fair than the centralization of power, control over information, and widening of the wealth gap evident in the world today.

Bitcoin's equitable governance shines a light on the uneven mechanisms of its fiat contemporaries. Through the conscientious empowerment of its community, it has established a thoughtful starting point for re-imagining organizational governance everywhere, generating questions and ideas about how to promote cooperation and achieve greater parity in all facets of society.

CHAPTER 10
FREEDOM

10.1 THE GOLDEN RULE

> *"When law and morality contradict each other, the citizen has the cruel alternative of either losing his moral sense or losing his respect for the law."*
>
> FRÉDÉRIC BASTIAT, *THE LAW*

Personal and economic freedoms are both based on the golden rule – the principle of morality that says to treat others as you would have them treat you. This means that everyone should be equally entitled to control their well-being and property, and, so long as they do not interfere with the rights of others, nobody should be deprived of them. Property in this case traditionally refers to money, real estate, collectibles, and other tangible assets, but in the digital age could be extended to include personal data and communications.

Bitcoin's framework for securely verifying proprietary data is staunchly supportive of these rights because it grants owners total control over their digital property. By enforcing the rightful use of money, Bitcoin removes the temptation of intermediaries, such as governments, who might find cause to violate our rights through morally questionable expropriation, taxation, or regulation.

Today, the responsibilities and benefits associated with the independent control of property are not widely exercised because we have grown accustomed to assigning oversight to third party intermediaries. We trust banks to protect our wealth and technology companies to store our data because they are regulated, convenient, or both. However, if we do not exercise our free rights and insist on their protection, we risk the moral decay that accompanies their abandonment.

10.2 THE DEPENDENCY TRAP

"Trusted third parties are security holes."

NICK SZABO, CYPHERPUNK, COMPUTER
SCIENTIST & LEGAL SCHOLAR

When we relinquish our property to third parties, it centralizes within their walled gardens, deepening our dependence on them and their influence over us because we must comply with their policies. Although regulations are meant to promote trust in their good stewardship, moral behavior is neither assured, nor dutifully enforced. All intermediaries are undeniably susceptible to misconduct, and with added influence at their disposal, they can exploit any perversions of morality on grander scales.

For example, in 2018, PwC estimated that global money laundering through banks totaled a staggering $1-$2 trillion,[25] accounting for roughly 2% to 5% of global GDP. Meanwhile, since 2000 global banks have been fined over $300 billion for misconducts, including money laundering, investor protection violations, sanctions violations, market manipulation, insider trading, and more.[26] So, why do financial crimes continue despite the industry being heavily regulated? In a word – incentives. Today, monetary penalties are not an effective deterrent. Instead, they have seemingly been embraced as a licensing fee for engaging in illicit activity. To wit, in a famous exchange from 2013,[27] US Senator Elizabeth Warren told JP Morgan CEO, Jamie Dimon, "I think you guys are breaking the law." To which Dimon slyly replied, "So hit me with a fine. We can afford it."

The technology sector is no different. In 2019, Facebook was fined $5 billion for personal data privacy violations related to its work with Cambridge Analytica,[28] and despite many other known instances of major data leaks and abuses, violations continue mostly unabated today.

10.3 HOME OF THE BRAVE

"Freedom and responsibility aren't interconnected things. They are the same thing."

HARRY BROWNE, WRITER & POLITICIAN

Circumstances may have been fertile for the growth of influential third parties in the not-so-distant past, but those conditions are changing. Concerned citizens and entrepreneurs with an eye on the not-too-distant future are creating tools that will allow us to secure property on our own terms, so that we may freely exercise our rights. The challenge in building these structures lies in formulating a strong alignment between the personal gains of builders and the social gains of users. Additionally, the challenge in maintaining their integrity lies in the need for sustained communal efforts to ward off those that would obstruct the rights they confer.

Bitcoin, of course, is the poster child of this movement. By decentralizing the responsibility for its maintenance (i.e. to miners, node operators, and developers), freedoms are enabled (i.e. censorship-resistant, trust-minimized data transmission) and communal benefits are secured (i.e. verifiably scarce and useful money), reinforcing the rationale to uphold it. As a potent tool for social and economic prosperity, it is inspiring new ventures seeking to propagate its virtues.

Take for example currency exchange Bisq, which facilitates peer-to-peer trade. Its code is open source and transparent for inspection, and its operations, including decision-making and revenue-sharing, are decentralized in order to remain self-sustaining and censorship-resistant. It is an organization with no owners and no headquarters. At no point does it act as a trusted third party to custody funds or store personal data. Instead, it matches trading partners for direct exchange to be carried out using security features embedded in the core functionality of Bitcoin.

10.4 CAPITAL CONTROL

"Bitcoin is a global phenomenon. An idea and a movement that represents a more connected and free world."

JACK MALLERS, FOUNDER OF ZAP

The advantages of using Bitcoin as sovereign money can be learnt by taking a single step. Whether it's experiencing the quiet exhilaration that comes from independently signing and verifying a transaction; or the latitude that comes from sending bitcoins across borders that fiat is restricted from traversing; or the relief of rapidly sending emergency funds to someone in need when traditional banking options are unavailable; or, perhaps, finding the peace of mind that comes from saving scarce and unencumbered money for the future.

These examples may not seem pertinent to those who enjoy greater civil liberties and relatively stable financial systems, but most people do not enjoy such comforts. Sadly, our world is littered with rigid economies that exert extreme financial and social controls, severely limiting personal property rights.

On any given day, money's accessibility could be tightly restricted through unexpected governance changes. Recent instances of money being held captive by central authorities include Iceland in 2008, Cyprus in 2013, Greece in 2015, and Argentina in 2019, among many others. In these examples, capital controls were implemented to restrict cash withdrawals, or limit and tax wire transfers crossing domestic borders. This ability to exert control over other people's money is the ability to deny property rights, which only accentuates injustice since it breaks the golden rule.

10.5 Moral Hazard

"With great power comes great responsibility."

STAN LEE, *SPIDERMAN*

The residual effects of the Global Financial Crisis have scarred the psyche of a generation by dramatically exposing them to fiat money's most dangerous fault – moral hazard. In economics, moral hazard is the detachment of cost from risk.

When the crisis struck, global central banks used their privileged powers to conjure hundreds of billions of dollars from thin air in order to purchase undesirable assets bound for the scrap yard of financial history. In doing so, the costs of failure, which should have been borne by the investors who freely took on their associated risks, were forced upon a blameless public. With that, risk was separated from cost, absolving investors of their mess, which got swept under the public's rug.

Actions like these are an abuse of power, which interrupt the restorative capacity of free markets to clear out ineffective ventures and sow the seeds for new ones to flourish. Had their artificially created money not been selectively doled out, many of the economy's imbalances could have been corrected. Companies that ought to have gone bankrupt would have, enticing surviving investors, entrepreneurs, and businesses to pick their pieces off the scrap heap, and then integrate them into more efficient and competent organizations. It undoubtedly would have been a painful process initially, but we would likely be better for it today.

Instead, because of our high time preference orientation and unwillingness to accept economic dynamism, we again traded integrity for expediency by letting central banks dictate the distribution of newly created money. In doing so, they unilaterally granted irresponsible enterprises a second chance to double down on their mistakes, stealing opportunity from the invisible hand of free markets.

10.6 AMORAL SAFEGUARD

"A wise neuter joins with neither, but uses both as his honest interest leads him."

WILLIAM PENN, WRITER & DEMOCRACY ADVOCATE

In Bitcoin, no moral hazard exists. No wizardry can compel unscheduled coins to come into existence or be spent unjustly. This system epitomizes freedom because it is both neutral, unaffected by biases or special interests, and also amoral, unable to accommodate even conscientious objections to the rightful use of property. Though the latter may be a tough pill to swallow, it is an agreeable compromise – a common ground – on which even adversaries can build trust and work together towards common goals.

The arguments supporting monetary amorality mostly align with those of Internet neutrality, except instead of contemplating the free flow of information, this concerns the free flow of value. The entirety of the arguments in favor and against neutrality, whether in the context of information or money, is the ongoing subject of debate around the world. While all sides can agree that it is desirable to prevent nefarious activity in both domains, doing so is a practical impossibility through regulation alone. Inevitably, bad actors will find a way to dodge rules like a good accountant finds tax loopholes, and well-intentioned regulations may inadvertently punish the innocent along with the guilty, callously trading precious freedoms for injustice disguised as security.

At day's end, all concerned parties should cooperate to deter immoral activity by calling attention to malicious behavior and defending each other's best interests, whether legislated or not. This high road is called integrity, and for a free society to achieve mutual benefits both allies and adversaries must find cause to care for its maintenance.

10.7 UNCHAINED

"Bitcoin is the spark that has reignited brushfires of freedom in the mind of mankind."

MILES SUTER, FREEDOM & BITCOIN ADVOCATE

Fortunately for Bitcoin, it is beyond the reach of overzealous regulators and authorities. It is virtually unaffected by legislation because it is perfectly functional, and also fully stateless, in both the physical and legal senses of the word.

With no physical asset to capture, *de jure* law – the type of law that governs modern society – cannot truly legislate the Bitcoin network. *De jure* legally recognizes and sanctions certain practices and conveys formal status, whether or not they exist in reality. For instance, current *de jure* law states that only fiat currencies are legal tender and therefore acceptable as money.

Bitcoin is governed differently though, by *de facto* law, meaning "matter of fact," since it operates independent of any state. Like math or gravity, its functionality is not subject to change, and it works regardless of any outside attempt to influence it. For example, despite Bitcoin having been temporarily banned in some countries, it continued working nevertheless as alternative money within those borders.

As a form of property that can only be managed by its rightful owner, which does not impede on others and cannot be obstructed by any third party, Bitcoin is the personification of the golden rule. It is an impartial, stateless, unrestricted, and unalienable property right, which, as sound money, could function as the linchpin of a sustainably free and fair society.

CHAPTER 11

DRAWBACKS

11.1 MIND THE GAP

"Avoid problems, and you'll never be the one who overcame them."

RICHARD BACH, AUTHOR

Without risk, there is no reward. This truism applies equally to Bitcoin as it does to most everything else in life. Given the very high stakes implied with Bitcoin, which amounts to nothing less than a complete overhaul of the conceptual foundations of money as we know it, the risks of this endeavor cannot be overstated.

Getting Bitcoin to where it is now has not been easy. It required herculean efforts from every corner of its community. Satoshi and all of the developers designed an incredibly robust and resilient network, but their work is nowhere near finished. Bitcoin entrepreneurs have built out infrastructure like exchanges, wallets, and out-of-the-box nodes, to transfer, store, and validate Bitcoin, but their work is nowhere near finished. Bitcoin's advocates contribute to a growing repository of educational resources about its technical underpinnings and economic principles, but you guessed it, their work is also nowhere near finished. All of this unfinished business stands as the chasm between what Bitcoin currently is and all the things it has the potential to become.

Up to this point, this book has romanticized Bitcoin, looking at it through rose-colored lenses, but in order to do it justice, a sober assessment of its shortcomings is also needed. Peering into the chasm of this unfinished business, this chapter will delve into some of the obstacles Bitcoin must overcome to realize its potential.

11.2 EASE OF USE

"The next big thing is the one that makes the last big thing usable."

BLAKE ROSS, CO-CREATOR OF MOZILLA FIREFOX

During the commercial expansion of the Internet in the 1990s, a router initially required a full minute or two to make a connection, jeopardizing a phone line in the process. Pages would load slowly, applications were rudimentary, and resources were sparse. The entire process was unfamiliar, complicated, and its usefulness limited. Today, the exact same could be said of Bitcoin.

When it comes to user experience, everything from learning about Bitcoin, to acquiring bitcoins, to sending and verifying a transaction, to opening a wallet, feels burdensome and problematic. It can feel even more complicated when learning how to secure your private keys, run a node, or become a miner, since improper use can lead to the irreplaceable loss of coins. These difficulties act as clear barriers to entry and adoption, especially in the absence of common knowledge about its benefits and best practices.

Although Bitcoin undoubtedly feels intimidating now, like the Internet before it, its auxiliary products, services, and applications are bound to evolve, abstracting away some of the complexities facing the average user, making its future use more prevalent and straightforward. Until then, however, it remains for the time being obscure and misunderstood, partially grounded as the next big thing waiting in the wings.

11.3.1 SPEED & SCALE: BOTTOM HEAVY

"The opportunity to build an enduring product far outweighs the cost of alienating a few users along the way. And the sooner you internalize that trade-off, the faster you'll move along the path to scale."

REID HOFFMAN, CO-FOUNDER LINKEDIN

Critics who focus on Bitcoin for its capabilities as a payment system question its ability to function as global money, since there is no known scenario where the core network can scale to handle billions of transactions per day or settle them near instantly, like Visa.

The reasons for this concern are legitimate. There are limits to the amount of data that can be stored within each block, limiting the amount of possible transactions that can be included, and, since blocks are only generated every 10 minutes, this is the minimum time required to settle a transaction. Also, practically speaking, the hard drive capacity needed to store all of the world's financial transactions would not allow the average user to run a full node.

There is no getting around this limitation given the current state of technology available to the average user. In order to preserve its ability to resist censorship, Bitcoin's most consequential feature, a trade-off was necessary. Limiting its throughput to ensure a high degree of security, Bitcoin chose integrity over expediency, sacrificing the possibility of operating at a Visa-like speed and capacity – at least on its foundational layer.

11.3.2 SPEED & SCALE: LIGHTER LAYERS

"Bitcoin itself cannot scale to have every single financial transaction in the world broadcast to everyone and included in the blockchain. There needs to be a secondary level of payments which is lighter weight and more efficient."

HAL FINNEY, BITCOIN PIONEER, DECEMBER 30, 2010

Just because Bitcoin cannot scale to satisfy the entirety of the world's transactional needs on its own does not mean it needs to. As censorship-resistant money, Bitcoin's foremost function is to secure money from interference by adversaries. Another word for protecting and preserving money is saving, and savings are not meant for regular transactional use – they are meant to be stored for future use. However, it is occasionally necessary to make a withdrawal from one's savings, like taking cash from a bank account.

The most promising mechanism for allowing more frequent cash-like transactions for Bitcoin is with second layer networks. The most prominent current example of this is the Lightning Network. If Bitcoin's base layer is freighter cargo, slowly carrying monetary value in bulk, then a second layer is local post, rapidly delivering lighter parcels. Second layer networks are a separate series of ledgers that record and consolidate many transactions, and then periodically settle them on the base layer like re-depositing cash back into the bank. It is likely that second layer networks will be able to handle significantly higher volumes of low-cost and high-speed transactions.

Though these technologies are still being developed and tested, and they are inherently riskier than the base protocol of Bitcoin, their carrying risks could be considered as acceptable as cash in your pocket. If they can scale to meet demand capacity, these complimentary networks could set a new cash-like standard for instant payments denominated in amounts as small as sats.

11.4.1 FULL CUSTODY: LOCK & KEY

"Not your keys, not your coins."

BITCOIN PROVERB

Despite its lack of physical state, it takes strong hands to hold bitcoins, and the only hands you should count on to ensure their security are your own. This can be done by taking full control of your wallet's private keys. In cryptography, private keys could be likened to the password for an e-mail account. Similar to how a password is needed to write or read messages from an e-mail address, private keys are required to send or access received bitcoins. All private keys are paired with a corresponding "public key" that, like the e-mail address itself, can be shared publicly in order to exchange proprietary data, be it written messages or bitcoins.

Regrettably, many uninformed and risk-seeking users tend to rely on intermediaries, which offer a false sense of security, to store or invest their bitcoins. From Mt. Gox to BitConnect to QuadrigaCX, and dozens of others, crypto exchanges and investment schemes that require users to relinquish their private keys have too often resulted in failure or theft, costing innocent users hundreds of millions of dollars. By pooling assets on large scales, these intermediaries are targets for bad actors that try to pry coins loose from weak hands, collecting whatever slips through the fingers of naïve or negligent users and businesses.

Whether by hook or by crook, every time there's an incident where bad actors abscond with other people's bitcoins, it leaves a black eye on Bitcoin's good name. This happens despite these incidents being completely unrelated to the performance of the underlying protocols.

11.4.2 Full Custody: The Burden of Ownership

"People often represent the weakest link in the security chain and are chronically responsible for the failure of security systems."

BRUCE SCHNEIER, CRYPTOGRAPHER

It would be a misconception to believe that Bitcoin itself has ever been hacked. Every instance of lost or stolen coins resulting from crypto exchange failures, investment scams, and other malicious activities are not the fault of Bitcoin. They are the fault of uninformed individuals, as well as bad actors who prey on the weaknesses of intermediaries and the people that operate them.

Given that Bitcoin's primary value propositions are its resistance to censorship and seizure, handing over control of your bitcoins to an intermediary, or in some other way relinquishing your private keys, defeats its purpose. And yet, these risky and avoidable behaviors are common for many users, suggesting that Bitcoin is still wanting for knowledge and resources regarding best practices pertaining to security.

If Bitcoin is to be universally adopted as honest and useful money, more users must take to heart the lessons from these past cautionary tales. The dubious track record of some of its shamefully departed intermediaries should motivate all users to make every effort to understand the cumbersome nature of private keys. Like anything worthwhile, locking down your personal Bitcoin bank requires some resolve, but this low hurdle is the only appreciable factor limiting anyone's pursuit and enjoyment of genuine monetary autonomy.

11.5.1 Dark Mode: Tools of the Trade

"The medium is the message."

Marshal McLuhan, Pioneer of Media Theory

At its brightest peaks, Bitcoin opens gateways that foster growth and progress, but in its shadowy valleys, it burrows tunnels that tolerate crime and indecency. A prime example of just such a hazard is darknet markets, which are anonymous, Internet-based black markets that sell or broker transactions for drugs, weapons, stolen credit cards, forged documents, and other illicit products. The most infamous example of this was the Silk Road, which was shut down by the FBI in 2013.

Some critics have taken issue with Bitcoin's complicity in crime, pointing to this as reason to ban it. This type of degradation is senseless though, because it is impossible for Bitcoin to prevent crime. It cannot differentiate between an innocent user and a thief, the same way a gun cannot choose if it is fired in defense or aggression. Signing a transaction with private keys is like pulling a trigger – it sparks a reaction, sending a transaction that, like a bullet fired, is irreversible.

Ultimately, Bitcoin's complicity in crime is no more offensive than that of banks in money laundering, since both are conduits used by law-abiding citizens and criminals alike.

Neither Bitcoin nor banks intentionally assist criminals, and, as noted in Chapter 10, their ability to fight or facilitate crime is not a matter that can be reliably deflected to regulation alone. The best way forward is to acknowledge that Bitcoin, like all money, is a mere tool, which both heroes and villains are privy to. Only by coming to grips with this reality can we have an honest discussion about the efficacy of monetary systems.

11.5.2 DARK MODE: FOLLOW THE MONEY

"I will love the light for it shows me the way, yet I will endure the darkness because it shows me the stars."

AUGUSTINE "OG" MANDINO, AUTHOR

Bitcoin will always bear the stigma of the Silk Road being one of its first real world use cases, even though it gave rise to the advent of law enforcement agencies learning how its complete, permanent, and public ledger of transactions can be analyzed to track suspected illicit activities. With help from specialized data forensic firms and organizations, such as the Blockchain Alliance, a light can be shined into some of Bitcoin's and other cryptocurrencies' darker corners.

Whereas traditional money laundering purposefully distorts paper trails by channeling money through many banks, legal entities, and jurisdictions, blockchains are a one-stop shop that transparently documents a complete ledger of transactions. If suspected illicit funds trade with known addresses, such as those of cryptocurrency exchanges, it's like leaving the flashers on an illegally parked car. It might as well shout out to law enforcement, "I'm committing a crime, and I'm right here!"

Over time, software proposals such as Schnorr Signatures and Taproot, and practices such as CoinJoin, which are all different approaches to disguising and mixing transactions, are likely to improve Bitcoin's privacy. These developments are not meant to stifle law enforcement agencies, nor are they meant as an invitation for criminals. They are merely digital extensions of the universal human rights to privacy and free expression (computer code is generally considered a type of communication), and as protection against the overreaching arms of institutional surveillance apparatuses.

11.5.3 DARK MODE: CHOKE POINTS & OLIVE BRANCHES

"Our arrows will blot out the sun ...
– Then we will fight in the shade."

FRANK MILLER & LYNN VARLEY, *300*

The right to personal privacy might be less contentious if it was more abundant, but today it is plainly in short supply. The distressing growth and social acceptance of technology-based data collection encroaches on and judges that which was formerly private. If Bitcoin makes genuine headway towards achieving privacy, the world might have a chance to restore its abundance and rediscover its benefits.

Conversely, if social derision and fear of the unknown overwhelms human rights principles as they relate to privacy, then the long arm of the law may try to threaten Bitcoin. Legal constraints on key infrastructure and onerous tax implications could constrain network activity and the livelihood of its users, relegating Bitcoin to the doldrums of black markets. Exchanges and miners, which have grown into full-fledged industries, currently interact with legacy banking and energy systems. If regulations were to prevent access to those resources, they could destroy businesses larger than those of home hobbyists. If those regulations were coordinated and imposed on a global scale, that could squeeze Bitcoin's liquidity, and weaken network security.

Although this worst-case scenario is very unlikely since many countries have generally been welcoming to Bitcoin, that is not the case everywhere. A few countries have imposed severe restrictions, highlighting the need for constructive dialogue and advocacy, like that offered by Coin Center in the US, which promotes sensible regulation by collaborating with governments and media, sharing research and educating them on related policy and rights issues.

11.6.1 MINING: CONSPICUOUS CONSUMPTION

*"Everything we hear is an opinion, not a fact.
Everything we see is a perspective, not the truth."*

MARCUS AURELIUS, ROMAN EMPEROR
& STOIC PHILOSOPHER

Bitcoin mining's energy consumption is a minefield for debate because it may be perceived as a detriment to the environment, and reliable data on the subject can be hard to come by. For some critics, its voracious appetite, which is estimated to have consumed 0.3% of global energy in 2019,[29] is frivolous and causes unnecessary environmental damage in the production of a luxury for those fortunate few who benefit from its monetary value. Considered in isolation, this perspective discounts the social gains of a Bitcoin-based monetary system, not to mention the impetus for miners to generate energy efficiencies and the complexity of the broader energy landscape.

Consider for a moment the phones, tablets, and other devices that we've become addicted to for constant communication and entertainment. Their planned obsolescence is insidiously wasteful, and they consume enormous amounts of energy, which is far more frivolous than Bitcoin. For instance, the most popular music video of 2019 used as much energy as 40,000 US households after hitting a record of 5 billion views on YouTube.[30] Meanwhile, the data centers that store and share those videos consumed 2% of worldwide electricity, and their appetite is expected to grow at least four-fold over the coming decade.

This information is not presented as a defense of Bitcoin's energy use, but merely to suggest that concerns for our carbon footprint should be considered in its broadest scope. Without question, Bitcoin has a large and growing demand for energy, but for all that it takes, you may be surprised to learn that it also has meaningful ways of giving back.

11.6.2 MINING: ENERGY EFFICIENCY

"To truly transform our economy, protect our security, and save our planet from the ravages of climate change, we need to ultimately make clean, renewable energy the profitable kind of energy."

BARACK OBAMA, 44TH PRESIDENT
OF THE UNITED STATES

Miners have clear motivation to reduce their energy consumption, since energy comes at a cost. As a result, they work to create more efficient equipment and, with few infrastructure needs, they can operate just about anywhere. This gives miners the flexibility to seek out energy sources that might otherwise be wasted. For example, a new business model uses Bitcoin to solve for gas flaring, which is the practice of burning off excess natural gas. In 2018 the World Bank estimated that flaring wasted 145 billion cubic meters of gas, which is equivalent to the annual gas consumption of Central and South America.[31] With Bitcoin, instead of being wasted, that gas can be converted into electricity on-site and consumed for a win-win scenario that subsidizes an environmentally friendly energy solution while securing the Bitcoin network.

According to the December 2019 Mining Update from CoinShares, a digital asset management firm, major mining operations are currently situated in regions with large, unused supplies of renewable energy because they tend to operate below peak capacity.[32] This aligns with miners' incentive to use energy efficiently, and also unlocks value from previously uneconomical renewable sources. Despite the report concluding that 73% of mining energy is derived from renewable sources, critics remind us that correlation does not imply causation.[33] Some renewable energy sources can only provide energy on an intermittent basis, but mining tends to require a constant flow. As a result, it is possible that some miners may have a partial need for "dirty" energy, despite any best laid plans.

11.6.3 MINING: OF CENTRAL CONCERN

"If you know the enemy and know yourself, you need not fear the result of a hundred battles."

SUN TZU, THE ART OF WAR

Although energy efficiency is undoubtedly a goal of Bitcoin mining, and it appears to be making progress in that regard, its level of consumption is a sticking point for some critics. To overcome their trepidation, more evidence may be needed proving beyond question that Bitcoin is not a drag on energy efficiency, but a driver of it.

Alas, energy consumption is just one of several elephants in the crowded room of concern for mining. Another is its current geographic concentration in China. As per the aforementioned CoinShares report, 65% of global hashrate (measure of computing power) is physically located there, with 54% alone located in the Sichuan region. It is also believed that mining pools, which allow independent miners anywhere to pool their hashrate and proportionately share block rewards, are equally, if not more heavily, based in China.

Having over half of all mining activity within the borders of any country, let alone a single region, is fundamentally unsound because centralization runs counter to Bitcoin ideology. It narrows the attack surface for a single adversary to seize a 51%+ majority stake in block creation. Although the likelihood of this type of attack is extremely low because there is almost no benefit to be gained and the resources required to sustain it would be untenable, if it were actually perpetrated, it would temporarily jeopardize transaction verification. At worst this could displace a couple blocks worth of coins, causing some reputational damage to Bitcoin, but the network would surely survive intact.

11.6.4 MINING: LAST LINE OF DEFENSE

"Time discovers truth."

LUCIUS ANNAEUS SENECA, ROMAN
STOIC PHILOSOPHER

Recent plans for major mining facilities to be built in other jurisdictions such as Canada, Russia, and the US give reason for optimism when it comes to increasing the decentralization of mining activity. However, there are still more mining concerns lurking on the horizon, namely the sustainability of miner compensation and the resulting network security.

In May 2020, the block rewards paid to miners were reduced by half, from 12.5 to 6.25 bitcoins. This milestone event known as the "halving," which occurs roughly every 4 years, means that miners must sustain themselves on half as many bitcoins as before. Given that real-world energy costs are not affected, and assuming that all else remains equal, in order for miners to maintain their efficacy, some combination of energy efficiencies or Bitcoin's price must double. Since neither is a given, for better or worse, the halving assures that Bitcoin's economic and energy dynamics must periodically evolve.

As keepers of Bitcoin's high-powered security apparatus, miners provide an indispensable service. With their fixed earnings systematically dwindling before ultimately ceasing after all 21 million bitcoins have been mined, miners will grow increasingly reliant on transaction fees for sustenance. Whether or not transaction fees alone will sufficiently reward miners for the long haul is an open question and topic of debate in the Bitcoin community. As the first and most robust system of its kind, built to continue running indefinitely, it will take more time before a conclusion can be definitively drawn on this topic.

11.7 ON APATHY & ATLAS

"Never doubt that a small group of thoughtful, committed, citizens can change the world. Indeed, it is the only thing that ever has."

MARGARET MEAD, CULTURAL ANTHROPOLOGIST

A guiding philosophy of Bitcoin's success to date, if it can be called that, has been its adversarial approach. The most ardent Bitcoin proponents are defense-oriented, anticipating ways it may need to survive and adapt so it can renew itself time and again, like a phoenix rising from the ashes. So long as there is a community of contributors, Bitcoin will remain active in perpetuity, but lurking within this notion of community lays an obscure risk – what if we lose interest? What if the lures of sound money, freedom, censorship resistance, and trust minimization, lose their appeal? What if nodes and miners drop off the network, abandoning the responsibility to verify and store the ledger?

Improbable as this scenario sounds given that Bitcoin has a large and growing network of developers, node operators, and miners – not to mention an army of self-anointed figureheads parading their interpretations of Bitcoin's virtues all over social media – the reality is that the majority of users are unlikely to run a node or miner. Whether due to technical ineptitude or lack of motivation, these users depend on others to hold the network accountable, and therein lay the rub.

Like Atlas, the Titan bearing the weight of the world, Bitcoin is, and likely always will be, reliant on a dedicated minority to diligently maintain the network. Of course, it would be unreasonable to expect absolutely everyone to be a miner or run their own node, but motivation to take up this mantle must spring eternal within the community if Bitcoin is to endure as sound money.

11.8 UPSET THE SETUP

"It's time for Plan ₿."

DAN HELD, HEAD OF BUSINESS
DEVELOPMENT AT KRAKEN

The fiat monetary system, with all its medieval practices, is at the very least familiar. Its institutions and policies have been around for many decades, and its results have been ingrained in us as socially acceptable. Exponential debt growth, inadequate savings, money printing, moral hazard, bankers' hours, excessive fees, unimaginative products, administrative inconveniences, outages, and errors are all part of the package that we tolerate because it is routine, and because we love to loathe it.

Vacating the ivory towers of legacy finance for an obscure electronic money might feel disconcerting, but it might also be worthwhile. Like a new language, Bitcoin can be difficult to understand at first, but with time and experience, it can become agreeable and, ultimately, preferable.

Though the potential risks and threats to Bitcoin are as many as there are oddities in Alice's Wonderland, all that can be done to protect against any undiscovered attack vector is to continuously be prepared. As an innovative, resilient, and collaborative network, Bitcoin has a wealth of tools and expertise at its disposal to solve any problem posed by the element of surprise.

This breadth of resources is the caveat to many of Bitcoin's pitfalls and shortcomings, because most of them have workable solutions. Even though the solutions may not be perfect and the work is unfinished, Bitcoin is already demonstrating that it warrants demand as sound money, and there's no drawback to having that as a viable alternative.

CHAPTER 12
OUTLOOK

12.1 MONOPOLY MONEY

"The game is rigged, but you cannot lose if you do not play."

DAVID SIMON, *THE WIRE*

Readers are likely familiar with the classic board game, Monopoly. As a reminder, the object of the game is to bankrupt your opponents by collecting rent, and buying and trading properties. In 2018, the game's maker, Hasbro, did a study that determined half of all players cheat.[34] Some of the most popular ways of cheating include bribing players with real-life rewards away from the game, stealing money from the bank, and stacking the playing cards to gain advantage.[35]

Ironically, there are a lot of parallels between the cheating strategies in Monopoly and the policies of central banking. When a central bank reduces interest rates, they are bribing you to take out debt. This cheap money offers instant gratification because it can be spent right away, but it comes at the cost of a claim against your future property. Another way central banks cheat is by increasing the currency supply, which is like stealing from the bank. In doing this, they line their own pockets with money that was not earned, artificially extending their ability to make payments and avoid bankruptcy. Lastly, when a central bank dislikes the card it draws, it can just pick another one. For instance, if a central bank has difficulty meeting its inflation target, it can either change the measuring tape, through substitutions and hedonic regression, or change the target, effectively re-shuffling the deck to get their preferred result.

Like sleight of hand, these policies deceive markets, resulting in the inefficient allocation of our time, effort, and resources. Without enforceable rules for money, central banks can continue breaking them, cheating us – the players who constitute the economy – out of a fair game.

12.2 THE DEBTOR'S DILEMMA

"You either die a hero, or live long enough to see yourself become the villain."

CHRISTOPHER NOLAN, *THE DARK KNIGHT*

The central banking system is a harbinger of uncertainty, directed by erratic central banks issuing fiat currencies that foster a myopic mindset for an economy inundated under a mountain of debt. To perpetuate economic activity, global markets have become increasingly and perilously dependent on fiat's anaemic policies. They inflate asset bubbles all over the financial landscape, failing to inspire the kind of fiscal discipline and behavioral productivity that ought to be expected of an efficient economy.

Under the mounting pressures of this dependency, and due to their sheer disregard for fiscal responsibility, world governments face two options for dealing with their debts – default or print. Defaulting on a national debt is like *seppeku*, the Japanese suicide ritual. It is an admission of grave error, and a penance to restore honor. This process is undoubtedly painful, but it allows for proper healing. The other option, printing money, is like a heroin addiction, because it draws out the suffering. Every hit provides temporary relief, but with diminishing returns. Each round of printing reduces the effects for the next round, leading to higher and higher doses, and ultimately, an overdose. Neither outcome is appealing, but most governments and central banks are out of options.

Regardless of how it happens, at some point these debts will come undone, and, with it, the fiat monetary system. When that time comes, in order to restore credibility to money and trust to commerce, the world will find itself in need of a new global standard.

12.3 FROM SAPLING TO SEQUOIA

"Greater than the tread of mighty armies is an idea whose time has come."

VICTOR HUGO, HISTORY OF A CRIME

A return to a sound monetary system is undoubtedly the best alternative, and Bitcoin is sound money by design. Guided by an unwavering set of coded principles, it sets a higher standard for money, allowing it to be saved without dilution, exchanged without interference, and safeguarded without trusting third parties. If adopted as a global standard, Bitcoin's insistence on the mutually beneficial ideals of freedom and accountability could alter the impetuses that drive our interactions, resulting in an improved set of communal priorities based on low time preference, collaboration, and resilience.

By putting an end to central banks, the golden goose of government profligacy would disappear. Central authorities would have to live within their means, just like the people they are meant to serve, equitably realigning economic incentives to favor those who create value, rather than those who debase it. Moreover, by restoring power to the periphery, the defense of individual property rights could be reinforced, alleviating enormous tensions that weigh on our social fabric.

It may be challenging to consider the notion that there is a causal relationship between money and civil society, but how could that not be the case when money is half of every transaction that perpetuates it? If we accept it as a truth that money and society are intertwined, then we should be extremely concerned with what we agree to use as money, for its ramifications are exhaustive. We should carefully evaluate all aspects of money to ensure that our chosen medium efficiently coordinates resources and promotes social prosperity, and we should consider the possibility that Magic Internet Money – Bitcoin – might just be best suited for this.

12.4 FORWARD GUIDANCE

"If we command our wealth, we shall be rich and free. If our wealth commands us, we are poor indeed."

EDMUND BURKE, UK MEMBER OF
PARLIAMENT & PHILOSOPHER

For far too long, it has been taboo to criticize our monetary system, despite it being one of the most crucial issues of all time. Control over money is an immense source of power – a *de facto* lever of control over the economy and, therefore, over all human action. Throughout much of history nation states have seized control of its reigns, corrupting it for political gain, but the faulty foundations of that authority are deteriorating before our eyes, like an incoming tide washing away castles made of sand.

If Bitcoin replaces fiat as the world's monetary standard, it could bring unprecedented integrity to society. It would dispel with the smoke and mirrors that have obscured the machinations of nation state money and insulated its authority, and, also, it would emphasize the powerful role of community in stimulating a righteous and productive economy. By ensuring that money remains sound and apolitical, it would function for the benefit of everyone, equally and without prejudice, revolutionizing our interpersonal values and opportunities for prosperity.

Considering that Bitcoin's total value is already greater than all but a handful of fiat currencies, it has already proven that globally agreeable money is not only valuable, but also viable at scale. Growing up alongside a generation whose commercial interests and skills are increasingly transitioning into the digital domain, and who have developed a justifiable mistrust of legacy monetary and banking systems in the aftermath of the Global Financial Crisis – economic, social, and technological trends all favor Bitcoin. As if designed to align with time, it pays respect to the past, lives for the present, and belongs to the future.

12.5 THE BOTTOM LINE

"You have brains in your head. You have feet in your shoes. You can steer yourself in any direction you choose."

DR. SEUSS, *OH, THE PLACES YOU'LL GO!*

Throughout this book, the interplays of cause and effect, risk and reward, and cost and benefit have all come into focus. To one degree or another, these reciprocal relationships are all a function of choice, which is reminiscent of one of the first lessons of economics – opportunity cost. This lesson teaches that every choice implies the refusal of another option. The associated cost of each decision is the missed benefit that could have resulted from the best alternative that was not chosen.

Bitcoin, as an alternative money, is unprecedented for the speed and scope with which it is revaluing the opportunity cost of pre-existing money everywhere. Its insistent presence in the global marketplace redefines money by demonstrating that it can exist independent of any state, that it can be compatible with time, that earnings can be commensurate to productivity, that credibility comes at a cost, that patience improves judgment, that precision fosters efficiency, that incentives outperform mandates, that utility is consequential, that proof builds trust, that justly empowered communities are resilient, that scarcity is a prerequisite of value, that competition drives growth, that adversaries benefit from collaboration, that good governance entails accountability, that equality breeds morality, that social consensus is scalable, and that responsibility is inseparable from freedom.

Of course, there is no grand plan for transitioning the world away from fiat and onto a Bitcoin monetary standard, just as there is no guarantee that it will fulfill any of its promises. There is simply a profound opportunity to make use of the only thing we can truly control – choice. If we can agree on the premise that Bitcoin is the most preferable money, we can solidify the ideals it epitomizes into the foundations of our socio-economy, unlocking extraordinary possibilities for our future. The catch is, you have to choose it over the alternatives, and nobody but you can determine if the cost it demands is worthwhile.

Resources

Bitcoin can be daunting because information is scattered, and not all of it is trustworthy. If you want to learn more, I recommend exploring some of the resources below. Please note that this list is by no means exhaustive because the Bitcoin landscape is always changing, and no single person or organization has all the answers.

The Bitcoin White Paper

https://bitcoin.org/bitcoin.pdf

Books

The Bitcoin Standard, by Saifedean Ammous
Inventing Bitcoin, by Yan Pritzker
The Little Bitcoin Book, by multiple authors
Programming Bitcoin, by Jimmy Song
Mastering Bitcoin, by Andreas Antonolopous
Bitcoin Money, by Michael Caras (illustrated book for children)

Full Node Solutions

Casa Node: https://keys.casa
Nodl: https://www.nodl.it
myNode: https://mynodebtc.com

Hardware Wallet Solutions

ColdCard: https://coinkite.com
Trezor: https://trezor.io
Ledger: https://www.ledger.com

Newsletters

Marty's Bent: https://tftc.io
Bitcoin Optech: https://bitcoinops.org

PODCASTS

Tales from the Crypt, hosted by Marty Bent
What Bitcoin Did, hosted by Peter McCormack
Stephan Livera Podcast, hosted by Stephan Livera

REFERENCES & ORGANIZATIONS

Bitcoin Wiki: https://en.bitcoin.it/wiki/Main_Page
Nakomoto Institute: https://nakamotoinstitute.org
Bitcoin Only: https://bitcoin-only.com
Bitcoin.page: https://www.lopp.net/bitcoin-information.html
Coin Center: https://www.coincenter.org
Bitcoin Resources: https://bitcoin-resources.com

JOIN THE CONVERSATION

A great deal of discussion occurs on Twitter, and it's currently the best place to engage with members of the Bitcoin community. To get involved, try following some of the accounts below as a lead-in to discovering the wider community.

@matt_odell	@pierre_rochard	@CaitlinLong_
@jimmysong	@francispouliot_	@wiz
@aantonop	@lopp	@starkness
@adam3us	@Melt_Dem	@JackMallers
@MartyBent	@bitstein	@dhruvbansal
@peterktodd	@pwuille	@RussellOkung
@6102bitcoin	@dergigi	@gladstein
@Breedlove22	@real_vijay	@BTCsessions
@prestonjbyrne	@saifedean	@milessuter
@jillruthcarlson	@danheld	@FriarHass
@hodlnaut	@AlenaSatoshi	@AlyseKilleen
@NickSzabo4	@theonevortex	@nwoodfine
@dickerson_des	@nvk	@parkeralewis
@LibertyBlitz	@TuurDemeester	@TheCryptoconomy
@stephanlivera	@PeterMcCormak	@coryklippsten
@nic__carter	@skwp	@jayberjay (my account)

As a Canadian, I feel compelled to apologize to the many amazing accounts that are not listed here. Sorry.

Finally, because Bitcoin is an idea, not a company, developers working on Bitcoin's codebase do so of their own volition, and sometimes without compensation. If you have benefited from Bitcoin, or would like to contribute to Bitcoin's advancement, please consider donating to developers at: https://bitcoindevlist.com.

ENDNOTES

Chapter 2: ORIGINS

[1]Satoshi Nakamoto, "Bitcoin: A Peer-to-Peer Electronic Cash System" (n.p., 2008).

[2]*The Economist,* "The trust machine: The promise of the blockchain" in the Leaders section (October 31, 2015).

[3]BitMEX Research, "Does Satoshi have a million Bitcoin?" (August 20, 2018) at: https://blog.bitmex.com/satoshis-1-million-bitcoin/.

Chapter 3: MONEY

[4]Established by Carl Menger, the father of the Austrian school of economics, and popularized by Ludwig Von Mises and his student, F.A. Hayek, among others.

[5]In 1971, former US President Richard Nixon undertook a series of economic measures to respond to increasing inflation. The most significant rendered inoperative the existing Bretton Woods system of international financial exchange. It came to be known as the Nixon Shock.

[6]Occurring between 2007 and 2008, it is considered by many economists to be the most serious financial crisis since the Great Depression of the 1930s.

Chapter 4: GROWTH

[7]Robert Breedlove, "Bitcoin and the Tyranny of Time Scarcity" The Bitcoin Times online (December 19, 2019).

[8]Evelyn Cheng, "Bitcoin debuts on the world's largest futures exchange, and prices fall slightly" CNBC: Markets online (December 17, 2017).

[9]Ryan Brown, "New York Stock Exchange owner launches futures contracts that pay out in bitcoin" CNBC: Cryptocurrency online (September 23, 2019).

Chapter 5: INNOVATION

[10]Vildana Haijric, "Bitcoin's 9,000,000% Rise this Decade Leaves the Skeptics Aghast" Bloomberg: Cryptocurrencies online (December 31, 2019).

[11]"Bitcoin's Security Model: A Deep Dive" CoinDesk online (November 13, 2016; updated February 22, 2019).

Chapter 6: RESILIENCE

[12]Accredited to Robert Metcalfe in regard to Ethernet, Metcalfe's law was presented in 1980. George Gilder expressed it in this form in 1993.

Chapter 7: SCARCITY

[13]Andrew Glester, "The Asteroid Trillionaires" *physicsworld* (June 11, 2018).

[14]Nassim Nicholas Taleb, *Antifragile: Things that Gain from Disorder* (Random House, 2012).

Chapter 8: COMPETITION

[15]Litecoin (LTC) was released via open-source on GitHub on October 7, 2011, by Charlie Lee, a Google employee and former Engineering Director at Coinbase. The Litecoin network went live on October 13, 2011.

[16]Zcash (ZEC) was developed by Electric Coin Company (zcashd) and Zcash Foundation (zebra) on open source. It was initially released on October 28, 2016.

[17]Ethereum (ETH, also known as Ether) was proposed in late 2013 by Vitalik Buterin, a cryptocurrency researcher and programmer. With its original release on July 30, 2015, Ethereum has an unusually long list of founders.

[18]Named after American cartoonist Rube Goldberg, this is a machine intentionally designed to perform a simple task in an indirect and overly complicated way.

[19]Amanda Russo, "Central Banks 'Waking Up' to Digital Currency, Create New Framework for CBDC Deployment with World Economic Forum" World Economic Forum (January 22, 2020).

[20]Nathaniel Popper and Mike Isaac, "Facebook and Telegram Are Hoping to Succeed Where Bitcoin Failed" *The New York Times* (February 28, 2019).

[21]Alun John, "China's digital currency will kick off 'horse race': central bank official" Reuters (November 6, 2019).

Chapter 9: GOVERNANCE

[22]"How Many Bitcoins Are Permanently Lost" Coin Metrics' State of the Network: Issue 26 (November 19, 2019).

[23]Lawrence Lessig, "Code Is Law: On Liberty in Cyberspace" *Harvard Magazine* (January 1, 2000).

[24]Hasu, "Unpacking Bitcoin's Social Contract: A framework for skeptics" medium.com (December 3, 2018).

Chapter 10: FREEDOM

[25] PwC's Global Economic Crime and Fraud Survey, "Fighting Fraud: A never-ending battle" (2020).

[26] See the Violation Tracker Industry Summary Page, specifying the financial services industry, produced by the Corporate Research Project of Good Jobs First at: https://violationtracker.goodjobsfirst.org/prog.php?major_industry_sum=financial+services

[27] Julia La Roche, "JP Morgan CEO Jamie Dimon once told Elizabeth Warren to 'hit' him with a fine because the bank could 'afford it'" Insider (March 31, 2015).

[28] Rob Davies and Dominic Rushe, "Facebook to pay $5bn fine as regulator settles Cambridge Analytica complaint" *The Guardian* (July 24, 2019).

Chapter 11: DRAWBACKS

[29] Nicola Jones, "How to stop data centres from gobbling up the world's electricity" *Nature* 561, pp. 163-166 (2018).

[30] Naomi Xu Elegant, "The Internet Cloud Has a Dirty Secret" *Fortune* (September 18, 2019).

[31] "Increased Shale Oil Production and Political Conflict Contribute to Increase in Global Gas Flaring" The World Bank online (June 12, 2019).

[32] Christopher Bendiksen & Samuel Gibbons, "The Bitcoin Mining Network – Trends, Composition, Average Creation Cost, Electricity Consumption & Sources" coinshares.com (December 3, 2019).

[33] https://digiconomist.net/bitcoin-energy-consumption

Chapter 12: OUTLOOK

[34] Mark Wilson, "50% of people cheat at Monopoly, so Hasbro redesigned it for them" *Fast Company* (May 22, 2018).

[35] Kirsten Acuna, "The top 10 ways fans say they cheat at Monopoly" Insider.com (January 16, 2018).

KEY TERMS

Bitcoin – a decentralized, distributed, peer-to-peer, digital monetary system. Created by Satoshi Nakamoto.

Bitcoins – [plural, lower case "b"] the monetary units of Bitcoin. Informally referred to as "coins."

Block – a data structure that records a set of transactions, typically occurring in 10-minute intervals.

Blockchain – a shared ledger or database that records data in blocks, which are sequentially bonded using cryptography, forming an immutable digital chain.

Block reward – a predetermined number of bitcoins that are systematically issued to Bitcoin miners as compensation for settling blocks.

BTC – the most common abbreviation, or ticker symbol, for bitcoins as displayed by the majority of exchanges, wallets, and merchants.

Code – a set of instructions dictating the operation of a computer program or application.

Consensus – agreement among network participants on program rules, data validity, and the overall state of the blockchain.

Cryptography – techniques for writing and solving messages using codes, especially to secure communications in the presence of adversaries.

Cypherpunk – activist advocating for the widespread use of cryptography as a means for social and political change, especially in defense of the right to privacy.

Decentralized – a sliding scale measuring the delegation of authority away from a single point of failure and center of power.

Distributed – copied and saved to many computers.

Fiat – an authoritative order or decree, often issued with impunity. As this pertains to money, it refers to a currency that is created at the sole discretion of a central bank.

Fork – intentional amendment to blockchain protocol. If changes are not agreed to via consensus, it is considered to be contentious, and can result in network fragmentation.

Halving – a periodic reduction of block rewards by half. Programmed to occur every 210,000 blocks, which is equivalent to approximately every 4 years. Rewards will cease once 21 million bitcoins have been issued.

Hashrate – a measure of computer processing power, expressed as TH/s, denoting trillions of hashes per second. Used to quantify mining intensity and network security.

Immutable – unable to be changed.

Liquidity – ease of convertibility for sale or exchange.

Mining – a competitive, computational process for generating blocks. Computational power is directly correlated with network security. Efforts are compensated with block rewards and transaction fees.

Monetary – relating to money.

Network – a series of connections between many computers adhering to protocols in order to facilitate voluntary interactions.

Node – a computer connected to the Bitcoin network, running its software to validate transactions, blocks, and protocol rules. "Full nodes" store the entire blockchain, the complete ledger of all transaction data.

Open-source – software released without copyright implications, where the owner grants anyone the right to distribute, use, examine, and modify its code for any purpose.

Private key – a secret access code used in cryptography to unlock data sent to a corresponding public key. In Bitcoin, it is required in order to spend coins.

Proof-of-work – a piece of data that is difficult to produce, but easy to verify. Discovered by miners, its inclusion in a block confirms that block's validity.

Protocol – standardized data transmission formats and processes, which form the basis of computerized communication and cooperation.

Pseudonymous – operating under an assumed name.

Public key – an address for receiving encrypted data, which can only be accessed with a private key. Represented by a string of alphanumeric characters. In Bitcoin, it is required in order to receive coins.

Sat – the smallest denomination of bitcoins. Expressed numerically as 0.00000001, or fractionally as one, one hundred millionth of a coin. Named after Satoshi.

Stablecoin – a digital coin whose value is pegged to or backed by fiat currency.

Stoicism – the sustained endurance of virtuous character; exemplifying courage, justice, moderation, and wisdom; highly composed and purpose-driven, even in the face of pain or adversity.

Utility – the state of being useful or beneficial.

Wallet – a software program or application for sending and receiving bitcoins by managing private keys, public keys, and transaction data.

ACKNOWLEDGMENTS

First and foremost, I would like to thank the Bitcoin community for their brilliance, which shaped many of my ideas, and for their passion, which inspired me to follow through with this book. For those who are interested in learning more about Bitcoin I highly recommend following them on social media, listening to their podcasts, watching their presentations, subscribing to their newsletters, and reading their books and blogs.

Thank you Ilia, for suggesting that I actually write this book. Thank you Alim, for being my sounding board since page one. Thank you Stephanie, for asking a very important question. Thank you Peter, for your honest assessments along the way. Thank you Miljan, for your diligent technical advice. Thank you Taheer, for your energetic feedback. And thank you Brian, for the fried chicken that jump-started my involvement with Bitcoin.

To my editor Catherine, thank you for bravely tackling this unfamiliar subject matter. To my interior designer Kim, thank you for your expertise and enthusiasm. To my graphic designer Daphne, thank you for getting out of your comfort zone and pouring your heart into your work.

Additionally, thank you to all of my family and friends for their encouragement, especially Kimi, for your impeccable attention to detail and boundless support, and my brother, for everything you do and everything we share.

Finally, thank you Satoshi, for giving the world a timeless gift.

Printed in Great Britain
by Amazon

53898723R00086